i

COUNTRIES THE AUTHOR HAS COACHED STUDENTS

U.S.A.

Australia

Belgium

Canada

Columbia

Denmark

France

Germany

Ireland

Japan

New Zealand

Norway

Sweden

United Kingdom

The Little Book of Answers to Life's Financial Questions

The 10 Core Principles required for achieving financial success and abundance

Written By:

Charles J. Machinski

Published By:

The Coaching Box, LLC

The Little Book of Answers to
Life's Financial Questions

1st Edition 2011- Unedited Original Material

COPYRIGHT©

Cover Design By: Dean R. Vigyikan
www.deanvigyikan.com

Photography By: Nicole Ekberg
http://photobynicole.blogspot.com/

WARNING – DISCLAIMER

This book was designed to provide information on the core principles the author recognizes as critical for financial success and personal wellbeing. These principles are the opinion of the author. They do not guarantee success as defined by the individual reader in any way shape or form. The content of this book is for informational purposes only. The author and/or third parties associated with this literary work including the publisher and distribution channels do not claim to be legal or licensed experts in any or all fields.

Success is defined and is the sole responsibility of the reader. The author, publisher, and distributors make no warranties or representation in the accuracy and completeness of the content and materials found therein. All efforts were made to ensure this work was accurate at the time of distribution to the public. It should be noted, in addition to possible error and omissions certain industry standards, guidelines and companies change. IRS rules and regulations also change. It is your responsibility to cross reference the information in this book with reliable sources to ensure its accuracy. It is also your responsibility to take charge of your life and implement the strategies that will take you to heightened levels of financial prosperity.

This book is not intended to replace competent healthcare or other professional advice from a licensed practitioner required for your personal development including but not limited to physical health, mental health, or financial management.

Congratulations on taking the initial steps toward success by purchasing this book.

CONTENTS

THE LITTLE BOOK OF ANSWERS TO LIFE'S FINANCIAL QUESTIONS

The 10 Core Principles required for achieving financial success and abundance

ACKNOWLEDGEMENTS:

This book is dedicated to the many wonderful people that have touched and blessed my life.

To my students: The teacher has been taught. Your questions and personal financial situations have allowed me to expand my knowledge base. You have been the pivotal chapter in my life that allowed me to bring forth this book. How grateful I am for giving me the honor of being your friend and mentor.

To my parents: For their unconditional love, friendship and examples of charity.

To my little girl Krystal: For just being you. Thank you for the years filled with laughter, hugs and love. I want you to know Daddy has always been my favorite title.

To my wife, Jamie: Thank you for your support and never ending encouragement. We are on a wonderful journey. I Love You!

Special thanks to Melissa Sonntag, Kristine Guthrie and Sandy Thornock. Your time and insights are greatly appreciated.

A NOTE FROM THE AUTHOR:

Congratulations on making this purchase!

For years, I have seen individuals and families pay thousands of dollars for specialized programs to assist them in areas of financial management and personal development. Yes, working with a specialist that provides you with the individual attention and direction you need is worth something, but not thousands of dollars! Besides, for most people these programs are cost prohibitive. Only a select few have the financial means to pay for the help they require.

In writing this book, it was my goal to provide the tools you need to achieve financial freedom regardless of your current financial situation or ability to afford costly programs. My specialized Empowerment Coaching™ is designed to be affordable so I can reach out and help multitudes of people find success and happiness.

The road you are about to embark on is designed to empower your life. A road I started years ago at the height of my own financial turmoil. Since then, I have taught people around the country and internationally the core principles found in this book. Principles you must follow in order to achieve heightened levels of financial success and abundance.

May you always find joy in the journey!

The Author

CORE PRINCIPLE 1

HOW TO ADOPT THE FINANCIAL CODE OF CONDUCT OF THE WEALTHY

Do you ever wonder what makes people rich? How do they manage their money? How do they invest? Probably, the greatest of all the questions you should ask is: What can I do to get my share of it? In your youth you were probably subject to misinformation about who America's wealthy truly are and how they acquired their fortune. In my adult years I carried a preconceived notion and belief pattern that started when I was young. You might have heard something similar from your parents or guardians. "They must have inherited their wealth", "Their parents must be loaded and helped them get their start" or "It takes money to make money". All of these comments helped shape my personal belief pattern. The underlying message of this belief pattern is that if you were not born to privilege, becoming one of America's wealthy is far out of reach and not an option. The secret is out. You are capable of accumulating mass amounts of wealth by adopting The Financial Code of Conduct of The Wealthy.

You are not destined to live a life of financial hardship along with the worries associated with not having enough money to survive. Choose to make positive changes now and reap the rewards of a future filled with hope, excitement, purpose and MONEY!

INTERESTING STATISTICS...
(In case you were wondering)

AMERICA'S WEALTH DISTRIBUTION:

The wealthiest 1 percent of families own roughly 34.3% of the nation's net worth.

The top 10 percent of families own over 71% of the nation's net worth.

The bottom 60% of households possess only 4% of the nation's wealth.

Source:

http://www.faculty.fairfield.edu/faculty/hodgson/Course s/so11/stratification/income&wealth.htm

ADOPTING THE FINANCIAL CODE OF CONDUCT OF THE WEALTHY

Plenty of research has been done to profile America's wealthy. In the New York Times bestselling book, "The Millionaire Next Door", authors Stanley and Danko have done a wonderful job uncovering the lifestyles of the rich yet not so famous. Among their research, they discovered people that hold great wealth live in modest homes located in average neighborhoods. However, their net worth is much greater than that of their neighbors. Further research also supports they are thrifty, frugal, manage their cash flow and invest money on a consistent basis. Other research indicates they do not supplement their income by the use of credit and they take the time necessary to audit their accounts. They also have a plan for achieving their goals and objectives. One of the most fascinating facts that was uncovered is most of them are first generation rich, meaning they are self made! So much for my preconceived notion that the wealthy come from money and it takes money to make money. We now have evidence that most of us have been led astray on who America's wealthy truly are and how they achieved success. If you have been carrying around untrue belief patterns like I have, it is time to awaken and adopt a new pattern of thinking. It is time to recognize that everyone has the capacity to achieve all their dreams and financial objectives. If the average person can accumulate mass amounts of wealth, so can you!

The first code of conduct you must adopt is be *Goal Driven*

The wealthy have a plan. They are organized and set goals on a daily, weekly, monthly and yearly basis. Make it a point to adopt this lifestyle. Having clearly defined goals will provide you with vision and clarity. You should never start a new day without having a predetermined action plan of what you need to accomplish. If you do not have set goals and a daily action plan, you will never arrive at the destination you desire.

The second code of conduct you must adopt is *Cash Flow Management*

You must be a good steward of the money you are already in possession of. How can you be a good steward if you do not have a full accounting of how your money is used? It is time to develop that cash management tool known as a budget. Now, at first glance, the words budget might not sound appealing. However, the wealthy do not view budgeting as negative or something designed to create limitation. They view it as a tool to ensure they are on track towards meeting their financial goals and objectives. If you think budgeting is negative or restrictive, then decide today to change your perspective. Once your perspective is changed, your feelings will change and you will do what is required to develop this valuable tool.

In order to successfully budget, you need historical data. Every month, our lives are filled with variable expenses and unexpected emergencies. In addition to the variable expenses, most of us are plagued with a number of fixed expenditures including car payments, mortgage obligations and insurance costs. The difference between these two categories is that our variable expenses fluctuate on a monthly basis and the fixed expenditures do not. Starting a budget is quite simple but requires discipline and effort. However, it will be well worth your time and energy as you take control over your finances beginning with this fundamental step. Decide today to start tracking your expenses. For proper management, it is important to separate your expenses into categories when developing your tracking system. This will allow you to recognize how much you are spending in specific areas on a monthly basis. Once a spending history is created and you have three or four months worth of data, you can formulate a budget with accuracy. Why? Because having a history will allow you to project your future needs.

As you go through the month, it is important to review all areas of your expenses searching for ways to eliminate items that are not necessary. Remember, the keys to accumulating wealth is not what you spend, it is what you keep.

Not much of a spreadsheet guru or looking for a cheaper alternative than costly software? Then go to www.charlesjmachinski.com and download a spreadsheet designed for this purpose.

The third code of conduct you must adopt is *Mastering the Art of Thriftiness and Frugality*

The wealthy are America's bargain shoppers. They never pay full price unless it is an absolute necessity. They also realize the more they spend, the more they chip away at their future wealth building capacity. When calculating lost wealth due to your purchases, it's not only the amount you spend for items that need to be taken into consideration. You also have to factor in the loss of interest if you took that same money and invested it over a specified period of time.

The fourth code of conduct you must adopt is *Operate on a Cash Basis*

If you truly desire to rid yourself from the burden of debt, you must start operating on a cash basis. (The exception to this rule includes a home purchase and a student loan) If you can't afford to pay cash for your expenditure, then you simply cannot afford the expenditure. The wealthy realize purchasing items on credit will only increase the cost for those products and deplete your net worth. How? Due to the high interest rates associated with credit.

Want to increase your net worth? Then purchase a home. Statistics show the average net worth of a home owner is almost $30k dollars more than a renter. However, there are some guidelines you must follow when venturing in this direction.

1. With the exception of a student loan, be totally debt free before you start looking for a property. This includes all credit card debt, personal loans and car payments.
2. Do not purchase more home than you can afford. Just because you qualify to purchase a larger residence does not mean you should. The bigger the home the larger the mortgage payment. Not to mention higher utility bills and maintenance costs.
3. Open an account and start saving for a down payment, even if it takes several years to reach your goal. The larger the down payment, the lower your monthly payment. Not only will a larger down payment make your monthly obligation manageable, you will save a ton of money on interest. If possible, save 20%. This down payment percentage eliminates the mortgage insurance required by the lender and could save you thousands of dollars.

The fifth code of conduct you must adopt is *Pay Yourself First*

The wealthy recognize the importance of investing. Living below their means allows them to invest money on a consistent basis. They are wise investors who generally invest between 15-20% of their household income on an annual basis.

The sixth code of conduct you must adopt is *Maximize Your Income Stream*

The wealthy are always seeking opportunities to generate additional income. They view their time as money, so they use it wisely seeking for ways to maximize their profitability. Many are involved in personal business ventures. If you are seeking to get rich, the time to act is now! Very few people get rich working for someone else. Decide today to make a change and start exploring the option of entrepreneurship. One note of caution: You should NEVER quit your job to pursue a business venture until the business has a history of financial success. Better yet, keep your day job and look at your new venture as an alternate income stream to supplement your financial well being. Looking for a great opportunity that will change your life? Go online and access www.ardysslife.com/jamiecm and click on "Start a Business"

SIMPLE MONEY SAVING GUIDELINES OF THE WEATHLY

1. Go to the grocery store once a week and bring a list. Purchase generic or store brand items and use coupons.
2. Do not shop hungry.
3. If you like a product and can't find a coupon, call the manufacturer and request they send you one.
4. Shop at discount clubs and buy in bulk. Be cautious! Not all bulk packaging is designed to save you money. Know what you are buying and how much it costs at regular store prices.
5. Do not shop at convenience stores.
6. Use discount bakeries for breads and other snack foods.
7. Shop without your children. Kids will tug at your heartstrings and you might get tempted to buy items you otherwise would not purchase.
8. If you are a senior, shop on days that offer discounts.
9. Just because an item is on sale does not mean you should purchase it. Only buy products that are needed and will be used.
10. Plan your meals around sale items.
11. Eat what you make including the leftovers. This will save you time and money.
12. When you shop, take the time to audit receipts before leaving the store. If a mistake was made, chances are it was not in your favor.

13. You can find slightly used items at garage sales, thrift stores, estate sales and church flea markets for a fraction of the cost.
14. Stay out of the mall. There is no such thing as window shopping.
15. TV shopping networks are only designed to sell you products you do not need. Do yourself and your wallet a favor, by keeping those channels tuned out.
16. Before you buy a product, see if you could purchase the same item on-line for less money.
17. Want to free up quite a bit of liquidity? Then downsize your residence. A smaller home means a smaller payment, lower taxes and costs less to run.
18. Do it yourself – Make general repairs without paying someone else to do them for you.
19. Buy the parts then pay for the installation. Most automotive repair shops charge a premium for the products they sell.
20. Do not make home improvements unless you own the property and pay cash. Too often people use credit or equity lines to cover the costs of remodeling. Doing this will only get you deeper in debt and cost more due to interest charges.
21. New purchases such as appliances and electronics typically come with a manufacturer's warranty. Do not let sales people rope you into purchasing a warranty.
22. Take care of your own yard verses hiring a third party. This would include mowing, fertilizing and gardening.

23. Grow your own fruits and veggies. If your harvest is more than your family can eat, learn to can and keep the items as part of your food storage.
24. If your rental property is not covering your expenses, dump it.
25. Stop drinking bottled water and soda.
26. Learn to do your own nails or have a friend do them for you.
27. Do your own hair or look for a cheaper salon.
28. Stop using expensive hair care products.
29. Look for cheaper skin care and make-up alternatives.
30. Wash your own clothes and make sure the washer is full before you use it.
31. Never dry clean an item unless it is worn more than once.
32. Use the dishwasher only when it is full.
33. Save on electricity. Use energy efficient bulbs and turn the lights out when you are not in the room.
34. Control the heat/air conditioning.
35. Buy energy efficient appliances.
36. When not in use, unplug your appliances.
37. Slow the flow: Turn the water off when shaving. Take a shower verses a bath. Conserve when watering your lawn.
38. Limit the amount of times you eat out. However, when you do, bring a coupon or go before the dinner rush and enjoy the early bird specials at a discounted rate.
39. Limit your entertainment expenses. If you are going on a date or having a night out with your

family, pick an option. Do not go out to eat and pay for an activity in the same outing.

40. When dining out, order water and skip the appetizers and dessert tray.
41. Brown bag your lunch.
42. If you go to a movie, pay matinee prices and stay away from the concession stands.
43. If your family likes to bowl, go during the week when the price per game is cheaper.
44. Look for free activity options and always bring a snack.
45. Stay out of snack shops including: Ice cream, coffee, bagel, pretzel, and cookie stores. Both your wallet and your waist line will thank you.
46. Meet your blind date at a coffee shop or bakery verses a costly restaurant.
47. Eliminate your cable TV or satellite service. If you decide to keep the service, then stick to the basic channels only.
48. Do not rent DVDs, get your movies from the library where they are free.
49. Love books? Get them at the library where they are free or jump online and pick them up for a fraction of the cost.
50. Reshop your communication services. If possible, get rid of a phone line or your cell phone service. If it makes sense to keep it, then stick to the basic package and dump the expensive bells and whistles.
51. Never use directory assistance. If you need a telephone number, take the time to open the phone book or look for the number on-line.

52. Want to get healthy and save money? Stop smoking, drinking or chewing tobacco.
53. Don't gamble. You have better odds of being killed in a car crash than winning the lottery. If you have adopted the "you must be in it to win it" mindset, then limit your spending to one ticket.
54. Car pooling can save money and the environment.
55. Purchase gas at the cheapest station. If your vehicle does not require a higher grade of gasoline, go for the cheap stuff.
56. Change the oil in your car regularly. This will help maximize your vehicles performance and save you money.
57. Re-shop your car insurance. If you find a reputable provider willing to offer you identical coverage for a lower premium, go for it!
58. Most people wait for the last moment, then pay full price when purchasing gifts for birthdays and Christmas. Shop off season and search for clearance items during the year for a fraction of the original cost.
59. Remember, fancy packaging does not mean better quality. It only means you pay more money for the purchase.
60. Don't supplement your holiday shopping on credit, only use cash. If you have a hard time budgeting for these expenses, most banks offer Christmas savings clubs. Open one and contribute to the account monthly to cover next years' expenses.
61. Do not wait to send in a manufacturers rebate. Get it in the mail promptly and receive the promised rebate you deserve.

62. If a sale item is out of stock, ask for a rain check.
63. Make birthday cakes rather than purchasing them at a bakery.
64. If you are craving a snack, make it.
65. Get a roommate and share the bills.
66. Shopping off season and browsing consignment shops is a wonderful way to enhance your wardrobe and wallet.
67. If you enjoy the newspaper, purchase the Sunday Paper only. Besides, using those coupons will more than pay for this expense.
68. Don't use ATMs. You can't spend money if you do not carry some. Besides, ATM fees are outrageous.
69. Never pay for personal checking. Shop around. Some banks and credit unions not only offer free checking, but provide a small interest rate as well.
70. Do not order personal checks from your lender without first doing your homework. Other options like using a wholesale club might save you money.
71. Always say no to telemarketers. Better yet, place your name on the Do Not Call List to limit these phone calls.
72. If you are in the market to purchase a home or investment property, look for a short sale. The time it takes to coordinate this type of transaction is far from short, but buying a property that already has equity value is well worth the wait.
73. Shop around for the best mortgage. Go with the provider that offers the lowest interest rate and costs. Shy away from adjustable rate notes and interest only options.

74. Contact your mortgage provider to remove the mortgage insurance premium if you have 20% equity in your property.

75. If the county accesses your property higher than what it's worth, then you are paying too much in property taxes. Coordinate with the assessment office to lower the value and taxes.

76. Don't join book, CD or DVD clubs that automatically send you an item of the month. Chances are you will not return it in time and they will automatically bill you for a product you never intend to use.

77. If you are looking for wedding ring, visit your local pawn dealer. You could pick up a diamond ring for a fraction of the cost you would pay a jeweler.

78. Find a hall that allows you to cater special events. This will not only save you money, but provide a greater choice in food options.

79. Coordinate to have your wedding reception in a park.

80. Have a cash bar instead of an open one. If you feel obligated to provide your guests with some form of liquor, some establishments offer a beer and wine option for a fraction of the cost of a full service bar.

81. If you are planning a trip, try to coordinate your flights on a Tuesday or Wednesday when they are the cheapest.

82. Whenever you travel and the airline is looking for volunteers due to an overbooked situation, take it! You can use the flight vouchers and possibly save hundreds of dollars on your next trip.

83. When flying, pack light and only take 1 bag with you to avoid overweight and extra baggage fees.
84. Take a shuttle instead of a taxi. Shuttles are cheaper unless you travel in a group and everyone could fit in a cab for less money.
85. Going on a family outing? Pack a lunch and take snacks with you.
86. Do not buy a non essential item that exceeds $75 unless you take 48 hours to think about the purchase.
87. Don't pay for expensive gym memberships. There are cheaper alternatives at community centers.
88. Be healthy and money wise. People spend hundreds of dollars on supplements. Compare product ingredients. Go for quality at the best available price.
89. If you enjoy a protein shake after a good workout, make them yourself for a fraction of the cost verses ready-made drinks.
90. Getting your education at a ranked state school verses a private institution could save you thousands of dollars every year.
91. Start early when submitting your financial aid application. Waiting until the last minute might limit your award eligibility.
92. Millions of dollars go unclaimed every year. Take the time to research and apply for grants.
93. Don't lend money unless you consider it a gift. Most people that loan money (especially to dear friends and family members) never get paid back.
94. Avoid late payment fees by always paying your bills on time. Better yet, set up an automatic bill

pay to guarantee your payment will be processed by the due date.

95. Bring your balance below the high credit limit and stop paying over the limit fees.

96. Always review your monthly billing statements and check for errors.

97. Contact your credit card companies and request an interest rate reduction.

98. Stop recurring charges on your accounts. People spend lots of money for products and services they never use or they do not need.

99. If you are disciplined and determined not to use credit, transfer existing balances to a 0% card and start saving money on interest.

100. Do not go to home parties where you are going to feel obligated to make a purchase.

101. Need a car? Let someone else take the rapid depreciation of a new car. Purchase a good used vehicle and if possible, pay with cash.

102. Save money on your monthly premiums by increasing your car insurance deductable.

103. Do not pay for full coverage on a vehicle that is not in use. Coordinate with your provider to change the policy. Better yet, sell it and use the money to pay off your debts.

104. Do not wait to get your car repaired. The longer you wait, the more it might cost.

105. Need new car tires? Take time to call around for the best deal.

106. Keep your tires properly inflated. This will not only save you money on gas, it will also extend the life of your tires.

107. Prolong the life of your tires by rotating them.
108. Switch to term life insurance. This type of policy offers a death benefit for your loved one at lower monthly premiums than a whole life policy.
109. Do not be over insured. A life insurance policy is designed to protect your loved ones that are dependent upon you financially. It is not meant to make them wealthy upon your death.
110. Use Flex Spending Accounts. This will allow you to pay for certain medical and dental needs using pre-tax dollars.
111. Purchase generic medications for a fraction of the cost verses name brands.
112. If you take a medication on a regular basis, see if your pharmacy offers quantity discounts.
113. For best prices, shop around for the lowest cost and consider using a reputable online or mail order prescription drug company.
114. Why let the government have your money interest free? Change your W-4 form and put more money in your pocket on a monthly basis rather than getting an annual tax refund.
115. Always ask for a discount when shopping.

ANSWERS TO LIFE'S QUESTIONS

HOW CAN I EMBRACE CHANGE WHEN I FEAR IT?

Do not fear change. Fear not changing and remaining in your current financial situation. Every time self doubt creeps in and you start to deviate from focusing on the daily tasks required to successfully achieve your objectives, consciously make an effort to get back on track. Visualize the end result as you defined it and realize it is time to let nobody including yourself stop you from achieving a financially successful future. By making a conscious effort, you begin to tell your subconscious mind to accept change. Once this happens, you will view change as positive experience.

IS THERE ANY EXCEPTION TO THE CASH BASIS RULE? YES

Real estate purchases and educational loans should be the only expenditures that could be made with credit. Credit can also be used in the event a "genuine" emergency arises and you do not have the cash on hand to cover the costs of the emergency. With these purchases, make it a point to use the credit card with the least amount of interest. Remember, purchases made on credit increase the cost of the item due to interest charges. So pay it off as quickly as possible.

WHAT SHOULD I DO IF I STOPPED TRACKING MY EXPENSES?

The answer is quite simple, start tracking again. Cash management is critical to your success. You need to know where your money is being spent. Recommit yourself and start tracking your expenditures again on a daily basis.

DO I HAVE TO GET INVOLVED IN A BUSINESS IN ORDER TO GENERATE WEALTH? NO, But...

If entertaining the thought of self employment generates a sense of panic then this might not be an option. However, having an extra income stream will get you out of debt sooner and allow you to accumulate wealth faster. Just calculate how much faster your investments would grow if you invested an extra $500-$1000 per month over the next 10, 15 or 20 years. The difference would be substantial! If after careful consideration, going into business does not appeal to you, then seek additional income through a part time job, alternate employment or advancement within your current company.

RESOURCES TO CONSIDER

Living On A Dime - www.livingonadime.com

CoolSavings - www.coolsavings.com

Coupons.com - www.coupons.com

SmartSource.com - www.smartsource.com

Centsoff - www.centsoff.com

LowerMyBills.com - www.lowermybills.com

BillSaver.com - www.billsaver.com

The Dollar Stretcher - www.stretcher.com

AbeBooks.com - www.abebooks.com

DealOz - www.dealoz.com

Partnership for Prescription Assistance - www.pparx.com

TIPS FOR A MORE REWARDING AND FULFILLING LIFE

BE ACCOUNTABLE

It is time to empower your life by holding yourself accountable for all that surrounds you. You are responsible for creating your happiness or sadness. You are also responsible for your poverty or wealth. You are accountable to your reaction to life's challenges. All that surrounds you at this moment is a result of your creation.

CORE PRINCIPLE 2

TIME IS NOT THE EMEMY, YOUR CHOICES ARE. ORGANIZATION: A PRINCIPLE THAT GOVERNS SUCCESS

Organization is critical for achieving and maintaining a successful life. Clutter is the outward manifestation of an inner turmoil. It only leads to feelings of chaos and negativity which is not constructive to our personal well being. How can you move forward and enjoy higher levels of achievement and fulfillment if you surround yourself with clutter? You can't! So get organized in every facet of your life.

TIME GENERATING TECHNIQUES

Do you run late to your appointments? Do you sometimes use time as an excuse for not accomplishing whatever is important to you? Do you often hear yourself state or tell people, "If I only had the time". Are you that person? Always in a hurry and not able to accomplish all you set out to do. The time for awakening in NOW! Remember, no more excuses. You deserve a more rewarding and fulfilling life. The following suggestions will add years back to your life.

A. **Stop watching T.V.** Better yet, sell it on e-bay and make some money. The Nielsen Media Report states the average person watches close to 4 ½ hours of television on a daily basis. Over the course of a lifetime, this could equal over 128,115 wasted hours or 5,338 wasted days. To put it into further perspective, this would equal over 14 years of wasted life. Think about how much could be accomplished during this time period if you FOCUSED on what was most important.

B. **Wake up an hour earlier.** The National Sleep Foundation in the United States maintains the optimal amount of sleep for an adult is between 7-9 hours. Studies have been conducted by a wide array of medical and educational institutions. Several studies have reported higher increases in mortality rates of up to 50% in individuals that sleep extended hours. What is the optimal amount of sleep a grown individual should have? My suggestion is 7 solid hours of wonderful rest. That along with a heart healthy diet and exercise program will rejuvenate you and get you prepared to start a new day. Depending upon the amount of sleep you require, if you wake up one hour earlier on a daily basis, every year you would gain an additional 15 days of time.

> **"Formula for success: Rise early, work hard, strike oil."**

> **J. Paul Getty**

C. **Make the most of your commute.** According to Gallups' Annual Work and Education Survey the American worker spends an average of 46 minutes commuting on a typical work day. On a yearly basis, assuming a 5 day work week, that equals 11,960 hours a year or 239,200 hours over a twenty year period. Use this alone time as constructively as possible. Organize your thoughts, plan your day, pray or listen to educational CDs.

D. **Tune out the radio and focus on something more constructive.** According to Arbitron, on average, people listen to the radio 21 hours per week. Granted, people that listen to the radio frequently multi-task. However, if we were to take 1/3 of this figure that would equal 324 hours annually. Think about the possibilities if you were to use this time to your advantage.

E. **Hang up the phone.** I'm not against reaching out to the people we love and care about, however we spend countless hours on the phone. Sometimes with people we see on a daily basis! In searching for statistics to get a better understanding on the amount of time the average person wastes on the phone, I could not find a reliable source. In my opinion, the hours we spend on a daily basis have reached record heights. People are constantly on the phone. I have even heard people chatting away in a bathroom stall! My guess is that we could easily save 1 hour on a daily basis if we limit our phone time. On an annual basis, this would equal 365 additional hours. Over a twenty year period, this would quickly add up to over 7300 hours equal to over 304 days.

F. **Limit the amount of time you spend surfing the net.** People spend hours on-line daily. Granted some computer usage is warranted and constructive however, a good portion is not. Surfing the net is not going to get you any closer to your financial dreams unless you use this time wisely. The net is a wonderful tool for educational purposes or creating a website to sell products or services. I suggest you only surf the net with an objective in mind and limit your usage to a specific time. Once you have accomplished your task or your time has expired, turn your computer off.

THE BASICS OF PLANNING

Now that you have freed up hours of your time by following my suggestions, the next step is to plan your day. Planning is critical if you truly want to accomplish your life objectives.

1. Plan before the dawning of a new day or before you go to sleep at night. Pick a time when your life generally quiets down and is less distracting. Whatever time you choose, be consistent and stick to this schedule.
2. Sit for a few moments and quietly reflect on your recent day's journey. Did you accomplish all your objectives or were there action items left undone?
3. Write down the uncompleted tasks that will require your attention the following day, or in the

future. Your list could include: Appointments, errands, household chores, family commitments and work related activities. Jot down EVERYTHING that comes to your mind including time for meditation, prayer and exercise.

4. Once your list is completed, decide which items are critical for your success. These are the ones you need to focus on.

5. Next, prioritize your list and number them in order of importance. If your list appears to be overwhelming, that is okay! Focus on the important tasks first and enjoy the journey that awaits you. (Besides, if you do not accomplish everything you set out to do, you will always have another day to catch up.)

CAUTION: Beware of procrastination or using time in a non constructive manner. Do not sabotage reaching your goals and objectives by filling your day with useless activities. For example, if you made a commitment to yourself to spend 2 hours a day building a home based business, keep that appointment. Do not allow yourself to become side tracked. Remember, we need to change our actions on a daily basis in order to experience a greater tomorrow. Doing the same ol' thing will only result in the same ol' outcome. If you want change, then you must embrace it! Remember, you deserve a more rewarding life. A life filled with peace, harmony, self worth, meaning, clarity, direction, love, and yes... MONEY!

INTERNAL CLUTTER REMOVAL

Your surrounding environment is a sure indicator of your mental state. As previously stated, you can't properly function if you surround yourself with clutter. Clutter diminishes your inner energy and motivation to accomplish your life's desires. How can you feel organized internally and excited about achieving your objectives when you wake up to an unhealthy surrounding? You can't! This type of a surrounding only promotes frustration, depression, uneasiness, and negativity.

Sometimes this external outcome is a result of what you believe about yourself. Clutter equals unhealthy beliefs. The more clutter that surrounds you, the deeper rooted some of your beliefs might be. As a child, you might have been told you would never be as good as a sibling or that you would never amount up to anything or measure up. Unfortunately on a subconscious level, you took this as truth and allowed it to impact your life. You must remember, what someone else thinks about you is not a fact, it is only their opinion. One of our greatest blessings is that we get to choose our beliefs!

If you do not feel like you are worthy of being loved or having a life filled with glorious experiences and wonderful opportunities, then you need to do some soul searching. Once you isolate your negative belief patterns, trace them back to where they originated from. Declare out loud that you are no longer a prisoner from that belief or the experiences that created it. If necessary, forgive your trespasser and yourself and finally decide to break FREE!

It is important to note this is a process that might not happen overnight. When feelings of despair and negativity rear their ugly heads, recognize its source and realize you no longer accept them as truth. Remember you are divinely created and a valued member of the human family full of potential and self worth. Know that you deserve and should accept every blessing life has to offer without limits!

To help you on your new journey of self empowerment, not only do you need to eliminate the clutter in your minds, but the clutter that is external as well.

EXTERNAL CLUTTER REMOVAL

Start by asking yourself a few simple questions. Are you organized? Is your home neat in appearance? If I opened your closets, dresser draws or your car trunk, would I find a chaotic mess? If the IRS asked you for your tax returns from 2 years ago, would you be able to produce them without hesitancy? Can you find your home office desk or is it covered in letters, paperwork, books or partially completed projects? If any of these questions ring a bell, it is time to get organized. If your life is in such disarray and this appears to be a daunting task, decide to tackle this project in steps. The following suggestions will help you eliminate your external clutter. Remember, being organized is a critical key toward success.

CHARLIE'S TOP 16

1. Do not feed into the situation by making it worse. If you use it, put it back in its proper place. Not sure where that place is? Then find one and keep it there until it is needed again.

2. Make it a rule to review papers/letters only once. If you do not need it, then throw it away. If you do, file it accordingly.

3. Do not have a file system? Then create one. A separate folder should exist for important documentation and billing statements including investments, insurance, legal paper work and credit card statements.

4. Too many statements stack up on kitchen counters waiting for a review that never happens. Audit your accounts for discrepancies on a consistent basis and challenge erroneous information.

5. Make your bed in the morning. This will provide you with a sense of organization and help start your day on a positive note.

6. Never keep dirty dishes in your sink overnight. Why wake up to a mess?

7. When you change, hang up your clothes or place them in the laundry basket. Too often people accumulate piles of clothes on the floor which is only reflective of the piles of negative beliefs we cling onto.

8. Keep your car clean and neat in appearance including the trunk and glove compartment box.

9. Clean out your garage and storage space and have a yard sale, better yet, give useful items away to a needy family or reputable charity.

10. Organize your closets and dresser drawers and make a commitment to keep them that way.

11. Dust!

12. Clean all the mirrors in your home including the bathroom. Besides, the toothpaste splatters are not only messy, but a potential breeding ground for bacteria. Yuck!

13. Remove the dirt from your windows. Keep the shades open and enjoy the sunlight.

14. Take time and empty out the clothes dryer when the cycle is complete. Too many people use the machine as a closet, rummaging through dry wrinkled cloths looking for something to wear.

15. Pick a time on a weekly basis reserved for cleaning the house, then stick with this schedule.

16. Clean your fridge. Throw out expired items and discard anything that does not look healthy enough to eat.

I have struggled with the above culprits in my own life. This section on external clutter removal might appear basic and not worthy of mentioning, but being organized has many advantages. Think about it. Can you really operate effectively when your external environment is full of clutter? Chances are you feel overwhelmed, negative and have the inability to think or desire to move forward with your life. Now compare these feeling to those generated when your surrounding environment is organized and clean. How does it feel waking up to a clean home where everything is organized and in its proper place? If your external surroundings are organized, you will think and operate more clearly and effectively. This will enable you to accomplish your goals and daily tasks quicker. Need one more reason? It will make you feel good. So make a commitment and get organized.

IT'S TIME TO DUMP YOUR UNHEATHLY HABITS

People through the ages have used a variety of methods to ease their stress. Living in our modern world is no different. A healthy habit is one that promotes physical or spiritual wellness. Something that inspires and makes you feel good about who you are and have the potential to become. These habits make you feel glad to be alive. They will promote feelings of health and accomplishment. The list could include daily meditation, prayer, walking, jogging, weight training and all acts of service and kindness. On the opposite spectrum, beware of unhealthy habits especially those that are addictive in nature. They are only destructive and counterproductive when striving to achieve the life you desire. Some on this list might include drinking, gambling, drugs, smoking, pornography and overeating. As you gain control over your life by getting organized both internally and externally you will automatically have more power to overcome the negative influences in your life and substitute them for something more positive. You will come to the realization it is time you dump your unhealthy habits that only chain you down. If you still find yourself struggling, then it is time to reach out and get the help you need. There are wonderful organizations set up to assist you and many are free. Go for it! And remember, you deserve a better life!

ANSWERS TO LIFE'S QUESTIONS

HOW CAN I GET MY SPOUSE OR SIGNIFICANT OTHER TO GET ORGANIZED?

Just like children, adults require structure. Sit down with your spouse and let them know the reasons why organization is important to you and what you are seeking to accomplish. Then create a list of tasks that need to be accomplished and decide together who is going to complete each task and when. It is important to have fun with this. Life is not meant to be too serious. In addition to listing the tasks that need to be accomplished, create some fun rewards the both of you could enjoy together. One secret for happiness can be summed up by the following phrase: Laugh often and love always.

HOW CAN I INSTILL THIS PRINCIPLE INTO MY CHILDREN?

Children learn by example. Be the example you want them to follow. They will emulate what is important to you. They also need structure in their young lives. Set specific rules and guidelines about putting toys in their proper place when they are finished playing with them and the importance of placing dirty clothes in the hamper. As children get older, they should be given a set of chores to do on a daily basis. This will teach them the importance of keeping their external environment clean and neat in appearance, which will serve them well in the future. It will also help foster the environment you feel comfortable living in.

HOW CAN I GET RID OF THINGS THAT HAVE SENTIMENTAL VALUE?

Do not be a clutter bug. "Things" do not provide us with sentimental value, but the memories from treasured experiences and relationships. Keep a select few items and give the rest to people who will appreciate them.

HOW CAN I EVER GET ORGANIZED WHEN MY HOME IS TOO SMALL?

Your home is not too small. Your collection is too large. Downsize your collection.

WHAT IF I DO NOT COMPLETE EVERYTHING ON MY DAILY PLANNING LIST?

Do not think you are a failure if you don't accomplish everything on your daily planning list. It could take longer to complete certain tasks than originally expected. Remember, we need to enjoy the journey in life. Any task not completed should be placed on your list for tomorrow's focus.

RESOURCES TO CONSIDER

1-800-GOT-JUNK - This organization is a full service junk removal company. They remove everything from old furniture to renovation debris.

1-800-SA-TRUCK - Dial this number to schedule a pick-up with the Salvation Army. Donations are greatly appreciated and could include clothing, furniture and other household goods. Besides, charitable contributions are tax deductable.

www.spacesavers.com - Can provide you with many ideas and products to help get your life in order.

www.shopgetorganized.com - This site offers a variety of products designed to create space and help organize your life.

www.NAPO.net - The National Association of Professional Organizers is available for people who really need help organizing their personal or professional life.

www.aa.org - Alcoholics Anonymous is a nonprofit organization. It is a fellowship of men and woman who share their experiences, strength and hope with each other to solve their common problem and help others recover from alcoholism. Access this website for information or to find a meeting in your local area.

www.na.org - Narcotics Anonymous is an international, community-based association of recovering drug addicts with more than 43,900 weekly meetings in over 127 countries worldwide. Access this website for information or to find a meeting in your local area.

- This website is filled with research reports, information and statistics. They have links to many useful resources including a section for teens and a clinic finder for those seeking help.

TIPS FOR A MORE REWARDING AND FULFILLING LIFE

FEAR: THE GREATEST OF ALL INHIBITORS

Fear is one of the biggest obstacles every person has the ability to overcome. Fear is absolutely crippling and can cause you to be immobile. This immobility or lack of action on your part will only suppress your dreams and cloud your vision of securing a fulfilling future. To prevail against this adversity, recognize your inner potential. You must learn to master your fears and press forward with faith and hope keeping your eye focused on a brighter tomorrow. When you do this, you become empowered and have the ability to accomplish any task you set your mind on. Do not fear change, embrace it.

> **"There is nothing to fear, but fear itself."**
>
> **Franklin D. Roosevelt**

False
Evidence
Appearing
Real

CORE PRINCIPLE 3

CREDIT: THE ROOT OF FINANCIAL EVIL

"Worry is the interest paid by those who borrow trouble."

George Washington

I remember how grown up I felt upon opening my first charge account. A JC Penny card at the tender age of 18! It was thrilling to get what I wanted by owning a piece of plastic which entitled me to purchase items without cash. Within a couple of short years, I chose to allow other retailers to jump on the credit band wagon and before I knew it I had a Macys, Steinbach and Zale's Account! Not sure what a young man was going to do with a Zale's jewelry account, but my younger sisters were happy recipients of gold and diamond gifts. All mine for the taking at over 21% interest. Fun? Absolutely! Until that dreaded day when the bill arrived in the mail and my creditors were seeking payment. Charging a few hundred dollars appeared to be harmless until I did not have the financial means to pay off the balances. Once school was back in session and my summer job remained just that, I found myself financially strapped. So what did this teenage boy do? I stopped making the payments. I mean, heck I had to eat!

Eventually the following summer came and I worked to pay off the debts, only to start the vicious cycle all over again. My younger brother joined the same university I was attending and we did not have "new" clothes for school. The solution? Charge it! And charge it was exactly what I did.

Not only did I graduate from college, but I graduated from retail accounts to major credit cards. By the time I was in my mid thirties, I had close to eight credit card accounts, (Most were maxed out) owed back taxes to the IRS to the tune of $12k, had a car payment, a mortgage and was still paying my educational loans which I deferred due to financial hardship more than once.

What was the solution? Refinancing! Pull out some equity and consolidate some debt. Did this move stop the madness? No! It only made matters worse. Since I lacked discipline, it was not long before my credit cards had balances again and I owed even more money on a monthly basis.

I finally realized most credit is an ill to society. The more debt we have, the more enslaved we become to our creditors. We allow them to take control of our lives, willfully trading them our peace and security for the stress and despair associated with financial uncertainty. Yes! Credit is evil if we are not disciplined and use it wisely.

INTERESTING STATISTICS...
(In case you were wondering)

Are Credit Card balances on the rise? According to an article posted in www.creditcards.com the mean credit card balance for U.S. households fell to $7,489 in the second quarter. That's down $7,788 or 3.8% from the first quarter of the year before. About 15-20% is due to the credit card companies lowering credit balances or closing accounts. However, the article failed to mention how much of this decline was due to the record number of bankruptcy proceedings recorded in that same year.

How many credit obligations does the typical consumer have? On average, today's consumer has a total of 13 credit obligations on record at a credit bureau. Of these, 9 are likely to be credit cards and 4 are likely to be installment loans. Source: MyFico.com

How much debt does the average American have? According to Experian, the average American with a credit file is responsible for $16,635 worth of debt, excluding mortgage obligations. (Source: US News and World Report, The End of Credit Card Consumerism)

What percent of students carry credit cards? Depending upon the source, these statistics vary. According to NellieMae, 76% of undergraduates carry credit cards. An article from creditcards.com indicated, 56% of all undergraduates carried at least one credit card in their name. (Maybe the difference is credit cards issued in the name of the student) Either way, whatever the percentage might be, I can sum up the answer to this question with two simple words. "Too Many"

How much debt are we in? According to an article posted in www.creditcards.com, consumer debt totaled $2.503 trillion. This amount has held steady as of 2011.

HOW TO SAVE MONEY BY LOWERING YOUR INTEREST RATES

Unemployment is near 10%. The Gross National Product has been slowly recovering over the last three consecutive quarters however, signs indicate a recession is still looming as the number of bankruptcy claims by individuals and corporations continue to skyrocket. Unfortunately, many people experiencing a loss of income might not have the financial means to pay all of their debt obligations. It does not matter if you fall into this category or not. You must negotiate. Follow these simple steps and start saving money. I have assisted many people with this process and have seen some cut their interest rates in half! It would be well worth the phone calls.

STEP NO. 1: MAKE YOUR TARGET LIST

Start by making a list of ALL your debts not just your revolving credit card accounts. Your list should include major credit cards, retail accounts, student loans, car payments, mortgage obligations, equity lines of credit, personal loans, signature loans, pay day loans, and every other debt obligation you might have.

STEP NO. 2: ACCOUNT DETAILS

Next to the name of the debt you should include the interest rate, minimum payment required by the lending institution, the balance owed on the account, the high credit limit and telephone number of the creditor.

STEP NO. 3: DOUBLE DIGIT INTEREST

After listing all the account details, take a highlighter and mark all the liabilities with double digit interest rates. I recognize that creditors need to make a profit, however all too often they seek to make their fortune by charging double digit interest rates along with a variety of other fees. Just like many of you, I also bought into their scheme that undermined my financial prosperity. The first winter season after I started a mortgage business, I was not making enough money to pay all my debt obligations. Upon receiving an offer in the mail, I decided to visit my local lending institution with the intention of applying for a personal loan. The process was quite simple and took less than an hour to complete. I filled out the paperwork, signed my name on the bottom line and walked out of the bank with a check for a few thousand dollars. When my statement arrived the following month, I was on the hook for a $115 monthly payment. Of course this did not help matters. I had trouble paying my debt obligations without the extra debt I now needed to pay. To make matters worse, the interest rate I was being charged was close to 30%! Only a few dollars out of my total monthly payment was being applied toward the principal portion of the balance. I was paying interest, and lots of it! When I ran the calculation, over $1200 that year went toward interest from this debt alone.

THE BOTTOM LINE: Interest is horrible, the more you pay the less you have. Decide today not to be a slave to your creditors.

STEP NO 4: DIAL FOR DOLLARS

Take your list and contact the creditors that are charging you double digit interest rates. Let them know you are experiencing financial hardship and need to speak with someone that might be able to assist you. Advise them the interest you have been paying on your account is not acceptable. Be firm and do not take no for an answer. If the initial contact you speak with is not capable of helping you, then request to speak with someone in management. If the phone call does not get you results, then call back at a different time and speak with someone else. By taking the time to contact your creditors, you will be amazed at how much this could potentially save you.

For example, most monthly minimum payments required by a creditor ranges between 2-3% of the outstanding balance. If you had a balance of $5000 and a creditor based their minimum payment calculation using 2.5%, the minimum payment requirement would be $125 per month. Based on the typical interest rates charged by a retail account, (lets' assume your rate is 22%) it would take over 72 payments to pay off the account in full. Now, let us assume the lender agreed to lower the interest rate to 17%. At first glance you might wonder if your effort was worth it. Let's run the numbers and see. At this new rate, you would pay the account off in a little over 60 payments. This would save you approximately 12 months of payments with an interest savings totaling over $1500! Talk about dialing for dollars! **THE BOTTOM LINE:** Every call you make is well worth the effort.

Dialing for dollars on revolving accounts is ideal however, not all creditors will automatically reduce your interest rates. For example, on a car loan or mortgage obligation the terms are fixed as stated in the note you signed at the time you secured financing. You might find the only way to reduce the interest on this type of debt is by refinancing. However, it does not hurt to make those phone calls and ask.

If dialing into your existing provider and speaking to a customer service representative does not yield the results you were seeking, consider one of these alternative options.

1. **Speak With The Financial Hardship Department** – Every company that issues credit to consumers has a Financial Hardship Department. They might call it by a different name, but they all have one. This department is trained to assist customers experiencing financial hardship. They are highly trained in the art of negotiation. Explain your situation. Let them know if something is not done about your interest rates and payments you might not be able to meet your obligations. Once they hear they might not get paid, they might be more willing to listen and help.

2. **Balance Transfers (New Accounts)** – If you have a good credit rating, explore the option of opening a new account with a different provider. I'm all for paying the least amount of interest. The less interest you are required to pay, the more money you will have to apply toward the principle

balance and eliminate the debt forever. Start shopping around for the best deal available. You want an offer with the lowest interest rate and the longest term available. (The term of the special offer should be at least 12 months) Also, look for an offer that is going to charge you the least amount in fees. Just a side note, if you open a new card, the credit inquiry will show up on your credit report for a 2 year period. For additional information and further insight on balance transfers, ensure you read my next section entitled: ON BALANCE TRANSFERS, YOU MUST BEWARE OF THE FINEPRINT.

3. **Balance Transfers (Existing Accounts)** – If you have an account that has a credit balance available, contact your existing provider and advise them you are interested in doing a balance transfer from other accounts to save money. Ask what type of offer they could give you. Get all the details including the interest rate, term and cost of completing the transaction. If you do not like one of these variables, then negotiate. It sure does not hurt to ask them for a lower rate or a longer term than what you were originally quoted. Once you have all the details, run the numbers and do what makes financial sense.

ON BALANCE TRANSFERS, BEWARE OF THE FINEPRINT

Creditors are not in business to save you money. They are in the business of making money off the interest you pay! When exploring credit card offers, make sure you take the time and review all the details of an offer including the terms listed under the fine print. Here are some of the items you need to be aware of.

A) Shy away from credit card offers where the interest calculation is compounded daily. This is a credit card, not a mortgage!

B) Stay clear of accounts that do not offer fixed interest rates. On these accounts, creditors offer a very low interest rate with the intention of luring the consumer. Once you are hooked, you are at the mercy of the lender and sky rocketing rates.

C) Do not fall into the trap of conditional accounts. Some creditors will provide you with a special initial interest rate, but on "condition" of using your charge card a couple of times per month. You need to start operating on a cash basis and some conditional accounts will not allow you to have that freedom. Besides, statistics show you are more likely to overbuy when using charge cards.

D) Make a payment on the account before the due date. This will ensure it will be processed on time. Better yet, set up an automatic bill pay so you never forget. If you are one day late with a payment, the low or 0% interest you are enjoying could shoot upward towards 30%!

E) Do not have accounts with companies that charge an annual fee. It is bad enough they sock it to you in interest.

F) Stay away from accounts that back bill you for interest if the account is not paid in full by the expiration of the special offer. If the interest clock is going to start ticking, let it start after your special offer expires or why bother opening the account at all.

HOW TO SAFEGUARD YOURSELF FROM THEFT

Identity theft has increased at alarming rates. To reduce the chances of identity theft and becoming a victim of fraud, follow these simple steps:

1. Do not leave your wallet or purse unattended. EVER! This includes places you think are secure.
2. Audit your credit and banking accounts on a monthly basis. Challenge all discrepancies.
3. When they are no longer needed, properly destroy statements or documents with your personal contact or credit information.
4. NEVER give credit card, bank information or social security information over the phone.
5. Make and keep a list of all your credit accounts including customer service telephone numbers in the event your wallet or purse gets stolen. If needed, request your creditors place your account on fraud alert. Doing this will freeze your accounts so they can't be used.

6. When ordering checks, have them delivered to your local bank not your home.
7. Monitor and alert the credit bureaus of suspicious or inaccurate information you find on your credit reports. You should monitor your credit reports on a consistent basis.

ANSWERS TO LIFE'S QUESTIONS

WHAT IS CONSIDERED GOOD CREDIT?

According to Bankrate.com, credit scores typically ranges between 300-850 points. The higher your score the more solid your credit history. It's safe to assume a FICO score exceeding 740 is excellent. (Not that this matters much since you are now operating on a cash basis! Correct?)

CAN I KEEP A CREDIT CARD FOR EMERGENCY PURPOSES? YES

But the card must never be carried on you and must only be used for genuine emergencies. It should be important to note birthdays, holidays, dining out or make yourself feel better gifts are not emergencies. Live below your means and eventually you could live above the means of most.

WHEN SEEKING A BALANCE TRANSFER TO SAVE INTEREST, HOW DO I RUN THE NUMBERS TO SEE IF SOMETHING MAKES FINANCIAL SENSE?

Compare the cost of what you have, verses the cost of what is being offered. First, you must take a look at the cost of the new offer. For example, let's assume you contacted a lender and the details of the transfer were as follows: 0% interest for 12 months and a 3% balance transfer fee. If you were going to transfer $3500 to the account, the calculation would look like this: $3500 X .03 (3%) = $105. This means the new lender is going to charge you $105 to complete the transaction. This fee would be added to the balance of the account along with the transfer. Next, you need to calculate the interest on your existing account for 12 months which is the term specified in the new offer. Now, most credit card companies calculate interest off the daily average balance but, interest calculations could vary. For purposes of this example, and to keep it simple, just take the interest you were charged on your existing statement and multiple that figure by 12 (Which is the special interest term of the new offer) Assuming your interest rate on your existing account is 21%, you would be paying approximately $60 per month in interest payments. ($60 X 12 = $720) Since it would only cost you $105 to do the balance transfer verses paying $720 in interest over the 12 month offer period, it makes financial sense to move forward with this transaction.

SHOULD I CLOSE MY ACCOUNTS WHEN I PAY OFF THE BALANCE? NO

If you close all your accounts, Fair Isaac who formulates the modeling for the major credit bureaus will not give you a rating. (Not that you will need to secure new lines of credit in the near future, however a healthy credit rating will be a requirement for purchasing investment properties when the time comes) You will find that some of your creditors will automatically close the accounts for you due to inactivity. When this occurs, it is a cost savings move by the lender. It costs them money to keep your account open and active.

SHOULD I CONTINUE TO DO BALANCE TRANSFERS TO SAVE MONEY? NO

Every time you coordinate to open a new charge account, a creditor is going to access your credit profile to help them determine the type of risk you are. The credit check a potential creditor makes is known as a hard inquiry. This type of inquiry will show up on your credit report for a 2 year period. Too many inquiries could damage your credit (FICO) score. If this was to occur, your existing accounts might use this as an excuse to increase your interest rate. Remember, they are in the market to rob you of your hard earned money and constantly on the lookout for any excuse possible to raise your rates.

I LACK DISCIPLINE AND GET TEMPTED TO USE MY CHARGE ACCOUNTS FOR PURCHASES I DO NOT HAVE THE MONEY TO PAY FOR. WHAT SHOULD I DO?

The answer to this question is quite simple, get rid of the temptation! You could start by destroying your credit cards. If you are tempted to purchase items you do not need, then stop going to the mall or watching TV networks designed to help you spend your hard earned cash. Make the decision today. Refuse to sacrifice the quality of your lifestyle in the years to come. Credit will only rob you of your dreams and enslave you.

IF I AM LATE WITH A PAYMENT, CAN OTHER CREDITORS INCREASE THE INTEREST RATE CHARGED? YES

When you first opened the account you signed a credit agreement. In the terms of this agreement you will find a "Default Rate" clause. This simply states if you are delinquent on a payment, the lender will increase your interest rate. Unfortunately, you do not only have to be late on their account for this clause to be activated. As long as you are late paying any bill reflected on your credit report a provider could increase the amount of interest they charge you. This clause is also commonly known as the "Universal Default Clause". In a motion to receive additional interest, banks that utilize the universal default clause occasionally check your credit reports.

CAN A CREDIT CARD COMPANY INCREASE MY RATE FOR NO REASON AT ALL? YES

When you originally signed the contract to open the account, most providers have a "Terms of The Agreement" clause included in the fine print. This section states the creditor could change the terms of the agreement at any time and for any reason whatsoever! This leaves you open to higher interest rates and payment levels at the discretion of the lender.

CAN I STILL USE MY CREDIT CARDS?

Research done by the American Psychological Association proves how you spend effects how much you spend. I have seen research that indicates spending using credit verses cash could increase the amount of your purchase by more than 20%! The bottom line is that people are more cautious of their expenditures when operating on a cash basis. Give your credit cards a haircut and operate on a cash basis!

To really apply the cash basis rule, you must stop using credit cards. Using them does nothing but chip away at your future wealth building capacity. It fosters overspending, and has you pay more for an item than what you would have paid if operating on a cash basis. For example, let us assume you purchased new stainless steel appliances for a total price tag of $4,500. Since you did not have the cash, you decided to open a charge account at the local appliance store. The terms of the account were 6 months no payment or interest. After the special initial offer period, the interest rate would be 19.99%. Be very cautious of these accounts. In most cases, if the balance is not paid in full before the special term expires, they will back bill you for all of the interest! Based on a 3% minimum payment on the outstanding balance, the total due on a monthly basis would be $135. Only making the minimum payment would take you over 4 years to pay off this debt! Total cost? $6,618. The difference between the original costs of the purchase against the cost if using credit, represents a total drain on your net worth of $2,118!

IS THERE A BENEFIT TO USING A CREDIT CARD WITH "REWARDS"?

Be cautious! Reward programs are marketing techniques lenders use to encourage spending. Do not fall into this trap. It only encourages overspending which equates to more debt and interest payments. My suggestion? Reward yourself by cutting up your credit cards. Remember, be committed and ALWAYS operate on a cash basis. If you can't afford to pay cash, then you just can't afford to purchase the item.

HOW LATE CAN I BE ON A PAYMENT WITH NO IMPACT TO MY CREDIT RATING?

By law, the credit bureaus can't report a late payment until you are 30 days late. Once this timetable is reached, your credit report will reflect the delinquency causing a downward adjustment to your credit score. (FICO Score) This delinquency will be reflected on your report for a 7 year period. So if you are in a current financial situation where money is tight and you are forced to juggle your finances, my suggestion is to juggle your finances in such a way to make the minimum payment on all accounts before they hit this 30 day period. Do not wait until the last moment to pay your debts! Once the money is received by your creditor, they have to process the payment which could take up to 3 business days. Waiting too long to submit a payment could put you past the 30 day mark. For every month the account is not brought current, your credit report will reflect this information. Ideally, you should try to make the minimum payments on your debts by the payment due date. This alone could save you quite a bit of money since most creditors charge a late payment fee that typically range between $30-40. In the event your late payment was a mere oversight, contact your creditor and request they reverse this fee. It is very rare they will not remove this charge if your account has a history in good standing. Remember, I'm all about keeping money in your pocket and increasing your net worth not your creditors.

HOW LONG DOES A BANKRUPTCY OR DEROGATORY INFORMATION IMPACT MY CREDIT RATING?

The Fair Credit Reporting Act section 605 highlights the requirements related to information contained in consumer reports. According to this document, satisfied judgments, tax liens and late histories could show up on your report for a 7 year period. Bankruptcy information could last for a 10 year period from the initial reporting.

CAN I STOP COLLECTION AGENCIES FROM HARRASSING ME? YES

The Federal Fair Credit Collections Practice Act provides consumers with protection from being unfairly harassed by debt collectors. This act typically governs and regulates collection attorneys and professional debt collection companies not the original creditor on the account. Original creditors are usually governed by state law. Most state laws mirror the guidelines covered under the act. This act says collectors are only allowed to call between the hours of 8am and 9pm. They are also not allowed to discuss your financial situation with third parties including employer, loved ones, and neighbors. The act also states if you request the collector not to contact you verbally, they can't. If a collector ignores your request not to be contacted verbally, send them a certified letter stating they are violating your legal rights under this act, and if verbal communication does not cease, you will file an official compliant with the Federal Trade Commission. (If you have been a victim and would like to file a formal complaint, contact your State Attorney General's office or contact the Federal Trade Commission)

IF I RECEIVE A LETTER FROM MY CREDIT CARD PROVIDER INDICATING THEY ARE INCREASING MY INTEREST RATES, SHOULD I OPT OUT? YES

When you choose to opt out this stops your creditor from increasing your interest rate. You will no longer be able to use the account for additional transactions and also agree the account will be closed once the balance is paid in full. This is a cleverly crafted ploy by the credit card providers. They know most people do not want to close their accounts thinking it will have a negative impact on their credit rating. Do not fall for it! If you have good established credit, closing one account will have a minimum impact on your rating. Besides, your rating will continue to skyrocket the more you pay down your debts obligations and stop carrying high balances.

HOW CAN I STOP USING CREDIT CARDS? IT'S EASIER THAN YOU THINK

This is not the question you should be asking. Instead, ask "How can I NOT stop using credit cards at the rates I'm being charged?" Make a commitment this very moment to avoid using credit cards unless it is for a required purchase and you have no other option. If the temptation is too high, get rid of the temptation! Give your credit cards a haircut. Operate on cash or use a debit card account. (A debit card acts like a credit card, but the cost of purchases made come directly out of your checking account) Making and keeping this commitment will help guarantee your financial success.

I FIND IT HARD TO SAY "NO". WHAT CAN I DO ABOUT TELEMARKETERS?

My suggestion is to put your number on the national Do Not Call Registry. Once your number is registered, it will permanently stay on the list unless you coordinate to remove it thanks to the Do-Not-Call Improvement Act of 2007 passed by congress in February of 2008. Once your name is on the list, creditors have 31 days to update their databases and stop harassing you. If they continue to call, advise them your number is on the Do Not Call List and request they stop calling you immediately. If calls continue, use the Do Not Call website listed below and file a complaint. www.donotcall.gov

HOW CAN I STOP PRE-APPROVED CREDIT CARD OFFERS FROM CLUTTERING UP MY MAILBOX?

I recall receiving over 15 credit card offers in 1 week! There are different ways your name and address might show up on a direct mailing list. Sometimes you provided your contact information to a company you have done business with. Other times companies pay to get a qualified list of potential customers from the credit bureaus! To stop the credit bureaus from selling your name, you can opt-out on line at the following website: www.optoutprescreen.com or by calling 888-5-OPTOUT.

If you want to slow the flow of all forms of junk mail, contact www.DMAchioce.org According to the Direct Marketing Association, marketers spent over $173.2 billion on direct marketing in the United States this past year. Measured against total US sales, these advertising expenditures generated $2.025 trillion in incremental sales. No wonder our mailboxes are overflowing. According to its website, the DMA is a global trade association of businesses and nonprofit organizations using and supporting multichannel direct marketing tools and techniques. Let your voice be heard and opt out.

SHALL I CONSOLIDATE MY DEBT BY USING AN UNSECURED LOAN? MAYBE

If you can save money by consolidating your debt into a lower interest rate loan, fantastic. But only do this if you are disciplined enough not to use credit once you coordinate the transfer. All too often, people use their charge accounts after a debt consolidation. Then they are stuck with additional obligations they need to pay off, on top of the consolidation. Just like a special offer from a credit card, always run the numbers and do what makes financial sense.

WHAT IS THE DEFINITION OF "DEBT TO INCOME RATIO"?

This ratio is calculated by dividing your monthly average gross income by the sum of all your monthly debt obligations. The higher the ratio, the greater risk you are to a potential lender. Lenders view debt to income ratios less than 20% as very good, between 21%-40% as good and between 41%-55% as fair. Anything that exceeds a 55% is considered poor.

RESOURCES TO CONSIDER

www.donotcall.gov or 888-382-1222- Use this site to register your telephone number and stop solicitation.

www.ftc.gov- The Federal Trade Commission is designed to protect the consumer. If you are being harassed by collection agencies, this website will provide you with instructions on how to file a complaint.

www.equifax.com or 1-800-685-1111- Equifax is one of the three major credit bureaus. Contact them directly to receive a free annual copy of your credit report. To place your file on fraud alert, contact them at 1-888-766-0008. You can also coordinate with them to dispute erroneous information found on your credit report.

www.experian.com or 1-888-397-3742- Experian is one of the three major credit bureaus. Contact them directly to receive a free annual copy of your credit report or to place your file on fraud alert. You can also coordinate with them to dispute erroneous information found on your credit report.

www.tuc.com or 1-800-888-4213- Trans Union Corporation is one of the three major credit bureaus. Contact them directly to receive a free annual copy of your credit report or to place your file on fraud alert. You can also coordinate with them to dispute erroneous information found on your credit report.

www.freecreditreport.com- This site can be used to access a free copy of your credit report.

TIPS FOR A MORE REWARDING AND FULFILLING LIFE

BE HUMBLE

Humility, as defined by the dictionary, is the opposite of pride and arrogance. To be humble is to be courteously respectful. It is a quality of meekness. Those that exhibit this characteristic are teachable. Being teachable is a sign of adaptability. You are not the master of all knowledge. Being humble is an essential quality to all those who want to achieve success in their lives.

CORE PRINCIPLE 4

BREAK FREE FROM THE BONDS OF SLAVERY: HOW TO RID YOURSELF OF TOXIC DEBT AND BECOME DEBT FREE

Every time you purchase an item using credit, it slowly diminishes your quality of life. Sometimes debt slowly creeps up on you, but eventually gets to the point where life can seem unbearable. You become slave to your creditors who reap the benefits of profitability at your expense. Sometimes in order to pay your bill, you are forced to work long hard hours at jobs providing minimum satisfaction and insufficient reward. You feel stuck, depressed and trapped. Life begins to lose its meaning and joy.

I have witnessed and experienced firsthand the devastating effects financial mismanagement can have on a person's emotional and physical health. People that have accumulated debt and experience difficulty paying it off on a consistent basis are often prone to depression, lack of sleep, anxiety and worry. Debts not only have a negative impact on your emotional wellness, but your physical health as well. Numerous studies have shown people that experience stress are more susceptible to disease.

Having excessive debt also causes havoc in relationships with family and friends. Since you are forced to work, the time required to nurture these relationships among all your other responsibilities make you feel like you are stretched too thin. Since the bills are always due, you sacrifice your time and energy forcing you to neglect certain areas of your life that provide some of the greatest joys in life. Statistics prove finances are also a major cause of disharmony between spouses or significant others. It also the leading cause of divorce!

It is time to break free from the bonds of slavery and rid yourself of toxic debt once and for all! It is time to bring meaning back into your life including the peace and tranquility that comes with debt freedom! Think of the possibilities! Having the financial means to cover your daily living expenditures and enough money left over to invest in your future. Imagine having the time to spend with your loved ones since you will no longer be chained to your office cubicle forced to work extra hours to meet your financial commitments. Not having debt will create the freedom and harmony you deserve and open up windows of opportunity and treasured life experiences!

INTERESTING STATISTICS...
(In case you were wondering)

Debt in our country is growing at a devastating rate; make a commitment today that your personal debt will not!

As of 2011, our national debt currently exceeds $14 Trillion dollars.

Over 8.5 Trillion dollars of our national debt is financed by foreign countries including Japan, China and the

United Kingdom.   Source: MSNBC article: "Just who owns the U.S. National Debt?"

It is also projected the U. S. Government will spend approximately $4.5 Trillion of your money on interest payments.

BANKRUPTCY STATISTICS:

According to www.UScourts.gov, non-business filings for the 12-month period ending December 31 exceeded $1.5 Million!   Experts agree this figure could increase substantially if everyone that needed to file could afford the filing fees.

Lehman Brothers Bankruptcy was the largest Chapter 11 filing of all time.   The filing included more than $625 Billion dollars worth of debt obligations and reflected more than 100,000 creditors.

BREAKING FREE: INITIAL STEPS

1. **COMMITMENT:** Decide today you are going to do whatever it takes to change your financial situation. Getting out of debt is a process that usually does not occur overnight. Be committed.
2. **RESPONSIBILITY:** Take responsibility for your financial situation and actions. You were not forced to make unhealthy decisions, you made them for yourself. Once you realize you are not a victim of circumstance and take

responsibility for your life, you will become empowered to make better choices.

3. **ASSESSMENT:** Be honest with yourself and explore the cause of your financial disharmony. Lack of money is never the cause. I have worked with people from a variety of professions whose income levels vary greatly. Many times physicians are in no better financial shape than a truck driver! Why? The more you make, the more you spend. It all boils down to your choices. Explore the reason why you make certain purchases and decide to change today.

4. **MAKE POSITIVE CHANGES:** At first this might require a conscious effort. Seek ways to minimize your expenditures. Take the time required to shop around. I recommend using "the rule of three" for all your important purchases. This rule requires you to research three separate providers for the products or services you are seeking. If all the companies are reputable, but one offers that same item at a lower cost, go for it! Remember, you want to increase your net worth by keeping money where it belongs. In your pocket! Another way to increase your net worth is to minimize your impulse buys. Any non essential item that costs over $75 should not be purchased unless you take 72 hours to think about it. During this time, consider the financial goals you have set for yourself and the impact this purchase might make on accomplishing them in a timely fashion.

You also need to question all your purchases. If they do not make financial sense, do not buy!

BREAKING FREE: BEHAVIOR CHANGES

1. **The Jones' are broke too** – Only a small handful of people hold America's wealth. Chances are the people you associate with on a daily basis are living far beyond their means. If they want to make continuous choices that only lead to financial disaster and unhappiness, love yourself enough and decide not to go along for the ride.

2. **Stop adult child care** – Once your children are raised, they are responsible for themselves. As a financial coach, I have seen parents subsidize their adult children's standard of living at the expense of their own financial security. I have witnessed parents going further into debt to pay daily living expenses including car and mortgage payments on behalf of their kids! Be honest with yourself and with others. If you can't afford to offer financial assistance, do not feel obligated to do so. You will be more of a burden on them in the future if you are not capable of caring for yourself financially in your elderly years. They have time on their side, you do not!

3. **Live below your means** – The secret to a secure and successful future is living below your

means and investing the difference. If you are struggling to survive, chances are high you might be living above your means. It's not a matter of what we make; it's a matter of what do with our money that counts.

4. **Stop using credit** – Decide today and start operating on a cash basis. Credit will only chain you down to a life of hardship.

5. **Never donate money that is not yours to give** -Generosity is quite admirable and I highly encourage it. If you want to receive abundance, I believe you have to give generously. However, you must have the money to give. Your retirement funds or other investment accounts are not negotiable. This is not your money. It belongs to your future. If you truly desire to help other people, you must first be able to stand on your own two feet.

BREAKING FREE: SUFFICIENT FOR YOUR NEEDS

You are under attack! Each and every day you are bombarded with cleverly disguised marketing tactics aimed at depleting your net worth. Retailers, financial organizations, car dealerships, restaurants and every other business have one goal in mind. To have you spend money and increase their bottom line. These organizations spend BILLIONS of dollars annually on mailing campaigns, radio slots, television commercials, billboards and every other marketing program you can think of. You are subject to hundreds of signals on a daily basis all sending out the same message. "Spend! Spend! Spend!" Your newspapers and mailbox become flooded with local advertisements featuring one day sales, semi annual sales, holiday sales, anniversary sales, end of season sales, weekend specials, mid-week specials, daily specials, inventory close out deals and going out of business sales. The sales never appear to end!

I recall seeing a car commercial featuring a beautiful middle aged couple looking to restore their youth behind a cherry red convertible. Yes, their life might look appealing and carefree, but wait until the car payment is due every month for the next 5 years. The joy of a new ride fades mighty fast when the bill comes due. I have also seen a commercial for a major credit card speak about freedom as butterflies dance across the screen. The only thing they forgot to mention was there is nothing free about using their card at a 24.9% interest rate. Do not fall into their trap! It is time to wake up, become aware and adopt a new pattern of thinking.

You must begin to distinguish between a need and a want. A need is a required purchase and includes essentials like food, shelter, clothing and transportation. A want is something we can live without. Yes, you might need transportation, but the need vanishes and quickly becomes a want if you desire an expensive foreign made vehicle you can't afford. Explore the reason why you want to purchase certain items then ask yourself if the item is a need or a want. Do you really need the purchase or is there something more economical and affordable you can purchase based on your existing income?   Do you have sufficient for your needs?   Once you realize spending excessive amounts of money only prolongs your ability at achieving debt and financial freedom, you will begin to second guess your expenditures.

It is important to note that wanting something is not bad if you have the financial means to cover the cost of the item without compromising your investments and debt freedom strategy.   Everybody deserves a life filled with better quality products and services, but you must be able to pay for them.   If you still have debt, you are better off delaying the gratification of a new purchase and reallocate those funds where it counts most.   On your bills!

BREAKING FREE: THE TOXIC DEBT SOLUTION™

The Toxic Debt Solution™ is a process to eliminate your debts in a quick and easy fashion.   The system is simple, yet has the potential of saving you tens of thousands of dollars in interest!

STEP 1: LIST ALL YOUR DEBT: It's important to note that a debt is something that can be paid off in its entirety.   This could include retail charge accounts, major credit cards, car loan, leases, student loans, personal loans, signature loans, mortgages and equity lines.   If you can't pay it off in full, then it does not belong on this list.   Examples of some liabilities that would not belong on the list would include car insurance, life insurance, utility bills and property taxes.

STEP 2: ACCOUNT DETAILS: Once your list is complete, write down the account details. Next to each debt, place the interest rate, the minimum payment due (as required by the lender) and the balance that is owed.

STEP 3: DEBT CALCULATION: Divide the balance due by the minimum payment requirement. This number will give you the approximate number of months/payments it will take to pay off each account.

STEP 4: THE SYSTEM: The debt with the lowest debt calculation number is your priority debt. With this system, you make the minimum payments on all of your obligations with the exception of the priority debt. This debt will receive the minimum payment plus any extra money available to pay it off the fastest way possible. This extra is also known as The Debt Destroyer Factor™. Once your initial priority debt is paid off, you add the minimum payment from this obligation to The Debt Destroyer Factor™. Doing this will increase your Debt Destroyer Factor™ allowing you to attack the next debt with greater force. Your next debt in order of priority would be the obligation with the next lowest debt calculation number. Just like I previously explained, you make the minimum payments on all your obligations with the exception of this one debt. This receives The Debt Destroyer Factor™ until it is paid off. After it is paid off, you take the minimum payment and add it to The Debt Destroyer Factor™. This causes it to grow even more allowing you to make a significant impact when paying off your next priority debt. This sequence should be followed until you are completely debt free! The process is simple, yet highly effective and can save you years worth of payments.

STEP 5: MANAGING THE INTEREST:

Interest is the only variable not taken into consideration in The Toxic Debt Solution™. Manage the amount of interest paid on your accounts. I'm all for receiving interest not paying it. Why make someone else wealthy? Besides, paying less interest means you will be debt free sooner.

BREAKING FREE: THE DEBT DESTROYER FACTOR™

As discussed in The Toxic Debt Solution™, the Debt Destroyer Factor™ is the extra money you plan to apply towards your priority debt. This money is derived in three different ways.

1. **Current Availability** - This is the positive difference between your financial inflow verses your outflow. In other words, it is the difference of your monthly income against all your monthly expenditures.
2. **Cash Flow Management** - Curtailing and eliminating your expenses is another way to develop The Debt Destroyer Factor™.
3. **Alternate Income Streams** – This money is developed through part time employment or a home based business. Always look for ways to increase your income!

Decide today and do what it takes to maximize this figure. Once you come up with a specific dollar amount you feel comfortable paying on a monthly basis, stay committed to this amount. Remember, the more money you apply towards your debts, the faster you will become debt free! Other money that can be used towards The Debt Destroyer Factor™ could include a tax refund, bonuses and monetary gifts.

ANSWERS TO LIFE'S QUESTIONS

SHOULD I INCLUDE MY MORTGAGE IN THE TOXIC DEBT SOLUTION™ OR KEEP MAKING PAYMENTS FOR THE TAX DEDUCTION? INCLUDE IT

Do not let your CPA mislead you! Dollar for dollar it usually makes more financial sense to pay off your property. You will pay the bank more money in interest than you will ever keep due to a tax deduction.

SHOULD I SET UP AN AUTOMATIC PAYMENT FOR MY DEBTS? YES

If your current employer pays you on a consistent basis, I suggest you use an automatic bill pay. Having an automatic bill pay is easy to set up and does not cost you an arm or a leg to do. Having your bills paid automatically will ensure your creditors are paid on a timely basis which means you will never have to worry about late payment fees being assessed by your creditors. This might also save you money in interest since your rates could increase if the minimum payments are not received and processed by the due date. To set up an automatic bill pay, first speak with your creditors. Some of them can coordinate and deduct the payment directly from your checking account on a monthly basis. If you have a checking or savings account with a lending institution that also carries the note for your car, credit card or mortgage, speak with your bank's customer service department. They would be more than happy to set up an automatic payment withdrawal from one of your accounts. Software like Quicken also has an automated bill payment service. For more information, you can access them online at www.quicken.intuit.com . Just click on the Quicken bill pay option under their products and services section.

DO I INCLUDE MY HOME IN THE TOXIC DEBT SOLUTION™ IF I DO NOT PLAN ON LIVING IN THE HOME LONG TERM? YES

Including it in the system will guarantee a net worth increase as you continue to pay off your mortgage obligation. I have seen countless people that had intentions of moving out of their homes only to remain there through their retirement years.

DO I INCLUDE MY BUSINESS DEBT IN THE TOXIC DEBT SOLUTION™ IF I'M SELF EMPLOYED? NO

Would you comingle your business and personal expenses? For IRS auditing purposes I sure hope not. Have a plan for both! Keeping it separate will help you maintain proper control over personal verses business debts.

SHOULD A STUDENT LOAN BE INCLUDED IN THE TOXIC DEBT SOLUTION™? MAYBE

Genuine student loans carry a very low interest rate. Chances are you can make more money in a long term CD or a Money Market account than the interest you would have to pay on this type of a note. If you can't make more money than the interest being charged, then include it in the program. Remember, your goal is to have your money work for you. So run those numbers and do what makes financial sense.

SHOULD I BUILD UP AN EMERGENCY FUND WHILE I STILL HAVE DEBT? YES

Before you start the Toxic Debt Solution™, you need to have between $1-3 thousand dollars in the bank to cover the costs of potential emergencies. I picked this figure since the mass majority of emergencies will cost under this dollar amount. I do not recommend you struggle to acquire a greater emergency fund at this time as suggested by a variety of other financial gurus. Besides, with the average debt load most people carry, chances are it would take you several years to reach a six month emergency fund goal. You are better off using the difference to pay down your debt obligations.

WHERE SHOULD I INVEST MY EMERGENCY FUND MONEY? DEPENDS

Your emergency money should be kept in a liquid account designed to provide you with the maximum interest gains. My suggestion is to place these funds in a Money Market account since they typically pays higher interest than a standard savings account. It is important to note emergency money should be kept in a separate account. Regardless of what you choose, you should never comingle these funds along with money from your primary checking account. If they are combined, you will use it!

IF I USE MY EMERGENCY MONEY TO PAY FOR AN UNEXPECTED EXPENSE, DO I CONTINUE TO USE THE DEBT DESTROYER FACTOR™ TOWARDS DEBT ELIMINATION OR REPLENISH THE FUNDS USED?

The money should be used to replenish the funds before applying it toward your debts. After they are replenished, continue attacking your debts following the system.

SHOULD I USE A DEBT MANAGEMENT COMPANY? NO

Never rely on a third party to fix your financial dilemma. During times of economic uncertainty these organizations feed upon consumer fears. Their marketing campaigns bombard the radio airwaves with all sorts of unrealistic promises. Some claim a quick solution to your debt woes promising you will only pay a fraction of what is owed on your accounts while simultaneously rebuilding your credit. Most of these companies do not follow through with what is being promised causing your credit rating to plummet. Why pay a third party when you can negotiate with your creditors on your own behalf. I prefer you to use the money towards eliminating your debts. Chances are very high you did not get into financial turmoil overnight, so do not expect a quick fix!

IS THERE A REPUTABLE DEBT COUNSELING SERVICE I CAN USE TO HELP ME? YES

Consumer Credit Counseling Services is a non-profit agency that was created in 1964. They have helped educate consumers about debt management, credit, and the consequences of bankruptcy. This organization offers assistance for people residing in all 50 states. For additional information, the CCCS can be contacted at 800-388-2227 or you can get further acquainted with the services they provide by accessing their website at www.cccsstl.org.

RESOURCES TO CONSIDER

bankrate.com- This website will allow you to compare online money market accounts and their respective interest rates.

TIPS FOR A MORE REWARDING AND FULFILLING LIFE

THE CALL TO ACTION

> **"Action is the foundational key to all success."**
>
> **Pablo Picasso**

This is a crucial step for anybody that wants to achieve success in their life. Procrastination is evil. It thwarts your ability and robs you of your future capacity to lead a happy and successful life. Not only is procrastination evil, but it will also sabotage the desired result you want to obtain and hinder realizing your life's objectives. If you are seeking a different outcome than the one you are experiencing, you must accept the call to action and do things differently on the road to freedom. The call to action is now. Do not procrastinate!

CORE PRINCIPLE 5

THE IMPORTANCE OF SEEKING ALTERNATE INCOME STREAMS

One of the biggest mistakes people make is relying solely upon one source of income. Having alternate income streams will provide greater financial freedom, but only if you use the money wisely. Think of how much faster you would be able to pay off your debts if you had an extra $300-500 per month to apply towards the Debt Destroyer Factor™. Chances are you would be able to shave years off your debt obligations and possibly save thousands of dollars worth of interest payments in the process. If you are at the investment stage, apply this dollar figure towards your investment strategy plan. Calculate how much faster you would be able to meet your financial goals and objectives if this extra money was invested consistently over a specified period of time.

The more income generated on a monthly basis once you have developed a debt free mindset, the more freedom you will experience. Why? Because you will be free from the heavy burden that comes with owing your creditors. Debt truly does enslave the borrower. It's time to remove the shackles and chains to which you are bound and break free! It is time to reclaim your life by following the Toxic Debt Solution™ then make wise financial investments based on educated decisions.

It is important to note, **MONEY DOES NOT CREATE ULTIMATE HAPPINESS**. It does create measures of it since we need money to survive and meet certain goals and objectives. Everyone's situation is unique. For example, if you are a young parent, never sacrifice developing and maintaining those treasured family relationships. These memories can never be recaptured. Getting out of debt a few years sooner by working extra hours or developing a business at the expense of your family relationships could have devastating consequences. You must seek balance in all things. Ensure you reserve time during each week to really maintain what is truly important in life. THE FAMILY!

I suggest you set aside at least one night a week when you can gather your family together to strengthen those relationships. On this day, all family members should know the importance of not coordinating any other activity except for the one that is designated and shared with other family members. My church community considers this day Family Home Evening. It is a time we all gather together for a meal where everyone is present with no exceptions. It is also a time used for prayer, scripture reading and a wholesome family activity. If you were to do this on a consistent basis, these precious relationships will be maintained and your children will know you have a sincere interest for their wellbeing. It will also help them make better decisions as they grow into adulthood. Doing this will not only nurture a loving relationship with your children, but foster a greater bond between you and your spouse. Not sure where to begin or how to coordinate an activity? Just Google "Family Home Evening" or access www.lds.org.

INTERESTING STATISTICS...
(In case you were wondering)

What is the minimum wage? The Fair Minimum Wage Act of 2007 increased the federal minimum wage to $7.25 on July 24th 2009. No additional adjustments have been made. Less than half the states have a minimum wage requirement above the federal level. Washington currently leads the pack paying $8.67 per hour. However, if you were to run the calculations, working full-time in Washington would only bring in an annual salary of a meager $18,033.

What is considered the poverty threshold for a family of 5? The US Census Bureau reports a 5 person family household where there are three children under the age of 18 has a $25,694 poverty threshold.

Where does your state rank in annual income by household? According to an article from the US Census Bureau, the following are the top 5 states with the highest and lowest median income based on a blended average.

HIGHEST MEDIAN INCOME:

1. New Hampshire $65,652
2. Maryland $65,552
3. New Jersey $65,249
4. Connecticut $64,158
5. Hawaii $63,104

LOWEST MEDIAN INCOME

1. Mississippi $35,499
2. Louisiana $39,418
3. Arkansas $39,452
4. Kentucky $40,029
5. Alabama $40,620

What is the median income per week? The median weekly income in the United States is $752 or $39,104.per year.

Over 50% of employees live paycheck to paycheck.

What is the unemployment rate? According to the Bureau of Labor statistics, unemployment has hit close to 10% of the US population. By state, unemployment varies with a maximum range of 14.3%. According to an article posted on CNNMoney.com, the recent couple of years have seen the greatest loss of employment in over 6 decades.

`

10 TIPS TO INCREASE YOUR INCOME IMMEDIATELY

Here are a couple of suggestions to maximize your income and increase your net worth.

TIP 1. Ask for a raise.

TIP 2. Look for opportunities for advancement within your company or firm.

TIP 3. If you are compensated on an hourly basis, work more hours. Let your boss know you are willing to work overtime.

TIP 4. Search for alternate employment with a higher pay scale.

TIP 5. Get a part time job.

TIP 6. Start a home based business.

TIP 7. Sell unwanted items on e-bay, Amazon or other online auction sites.

TIP 8. Acquire additional education. Many companies will give you a raise if you have an advanced degree.

TIP 9. Learn a trade and get a license. There are many options to choose from including nursing, plumbing, electrical, real estate, mortgage lending and appraisal.

TIP 10. If you are a stay at home parent, babysit someone else's child.

ANSWERS TO LIFE'S QUESTIONS

I HAVE BUSINESS AND PERSONAL DEBT, WHERE SHOULD I START?

Treat your business and personal expenses separately. Start with your personal debts first and pay them down in a systematic fashion following The Debt Destroyer Program™. If the business consistently loses money and has a poor financial history, get out from under it. Do not wait! Hanging on waiting for the tides to change will only get you further in debt and could spell disaster.

ARE THERE ANY TAX BENEFITS TO OWNING A BUSINESS? YES

The IRS allows contract employees and entrepreneurs certain tax deductions. Some of the deductions include vehicle expenses, marketing and advertisement costs, business related travel expenses, meals and entertainment costs and the home office deduction. Most of these expenses could be deducted dollar for dollar thus significantly lowering your tax obligation to the government. The only catch to these deductions: They must be business related! You can't take your family vacation with the expectation of writing off the trip as a business related expense. For additional information about the tax advantages of business ownership, access www.taxreductioninstitute .com. The Tax Reduction Institute was created by Sandy Botkin. Sandy is an authority on taxation and is both a Tax Attorney and CPA. He is also the author of several publications and offers an audio workshop on taxation called "The Tax Strategies for Business Professionals."

SHOULD I TAKE OUT A LOAN TO EXPAND MY BUSINESS VENTURE? NO

Going into debt with the hopes of increasing profitability thru business expansion is like going to Vegas and placing your money on a roulette table. Based on some of the statistics that exist, you might have better odds at the table. However, if your business is successful and you desire to increase your profitability through expansion, wonderful! But expand out by using your profits not by going into debt.

SHOULD I QUIT MY JOB AND FOCUS ON BUILDING MY BUSINESS? NO

I'm all for receiving multiple income streams. However, one of the biggest mistakes people make is they quit their day job prematurely. Until your business has been successfully bringing in a profit for over a year and prospects for continued growth and profitability are strong, do not give up something guaranteed.

WHERE CAN I FIND FUNDING TO START A BUSINESS? SAVINGS

Do not forget, your primary focus needs to be on eliminating your debts. If you make enough money to start a small business simultaneously, fantastic! But, do not start one at the expense of being debt free. If you still have debt, my suggestion is your little business venture should not exceed 4 months worth of savings. For a more costly venture, I recommend you wait until you are debt free. Once you are, you can take a portion of your monthly income and place it into an investment account. Continue to do this on a monthly basis until your financial goal is reached and you have the money needed to start a business.

WHAT TYPE OF INVESTMENT ACCOUNT SHOULD I USE TO SAVE UP THE MONEY TO OPEN A BUSINESS? DEPENDS

The answer to this question is going to vary based on the type of business you plan to open and the amount of money it will require. A franchise operation like a McDonalds might require a few hundred thousand dollars to start. Trying to acquire the liquidity/asset qualification determined by the franchisee could take many years. If saving projections exceed 10 years, invest the money in mutual funds. Mutual funds pose a greater risk since most of them are backed by stocks, but often provide a greater return than conservative investment options. If your potential business will only cost less than a couple thousand dollars to open and your saving projections is under a 5 year period, invest in more liquid instruments like CDs or money market accounts.

IS IT A GOOD IDEA TO START A BUSINESS WHEN I STILL HAVE DEBTS? DEPENDS

Before you spend money and venture in the direction of business ownership, ensure you have a $1k-$3k emergency fund. Do not use the money from this fund to set up a business no matter how small the cash requirement is. It is okay to start a business while you still have debt obligations if the business will not cost a substantial amount of money to start. Besides, the potential income stream generated could be applied towards your debt obligations and accelerate your payoff. While still in debt, the business should not cost you more than 4 months worth of savings to start.

SHOULD I USE MY EQUITY OR RETIREMENT MONEY TO START A BUSINESS? NO

Do not take out a small business loan or any other loan for business purposes. This includes equity lines or pulling money from retirement accounts. USE SAVINGS ONLY, NOT RETIREMENT INVESTMENTS!

I WOULD LIKE TO START A HOME BASED BUSINESS. ARE THERE ANY GUIDELINES I SHOULD FOLLOW TO PROTECT MYSELF FINANCIALLY? YES

Beware of so called "Business Opportunities" that cost thousands of dollars to start. Seek an opportunity that will cost a minimum amount of money to begin. You should never use credit cards, equity from your property or your emergency fund to start something speculative. It is also important to do your research. Many of these marketed businesses do not deliver what is being promised. Unfortunately, some are schemes. Part of doing your homework is to ensure an opportunity is legitimate. A good start would be to check with your local Better Business Bureau at www.bbb.org or www.bbbonline.org

RESOURCES TO CONSIDER

Home Based Business for Dummies, By Paul and Sarah Edwards

Network Marketing For Dummies, By Zig Ziglar

The Ultimate Small Business Marketing Guide, By James Stephenson

Multiple Streams of Income, By Robert Allen

Google: Home Based Business Ideas

TIPS FOR A MORE REWARDING AND FULFILLING LIFE

DO NOT MAKE MONEY YOUR GOD

A dear friend of mine has a wonderful expression he frequently uses. "We take the time for that which is important to us." A truly successful life, one that is personally rewarding, must be balanced. We must be cautious not to dedicate all of our time towards seeking financial gain. Your family, friends, being active in your local community, volunteering, and your relationship with God are essential. If you are seeking happiness in life, strive to strengthen these relationships. A quote made by David O. McKay provides us with a wonderful reminder on the importance of keeping the proper perspective. "No success can compensate for failure in the home."

"And in the end it's not the years in your life that count. It's the life in your years"

Abraham Lincoln

CORE PRINCIPLE 6

PART OF CREATING THE GOLDEN EGG IS BUILDING A NEST TO KEEP IT IN: REAL ESTATE AND MORTGAGE LENDING

Home ownership is one way for you to give yourself an annual pay increase. Yes, home values fluctuate depending upon market conditions, however a home is a long term investment and will appreciate in value over time. People that hold America's wealth do not rent, the mass majority of them hold property ownership. Owning real estate is a key towards generating wealth. But, does it always make sense to buy a home? What if you have debt obligations? What if a change in your income has turned your financial picture from bright and vibrant to dark, dreary and depressing? What if you can no longer afford your home and are facing foreclosure? How important is credit? How do you crunch the numbers to ensure an investment property makes financial sense? This section is designed to educate and help answer some of the most popular questions I have been asked about real estate and mortgage lending. One of the biggest mistakes a person can make is not purchasing a property. Even bigger is purchasing a property you can't afford. Be wise in all your financial decisions! This includes a home or investment property purchase and associated financing.

INTERESTING STATISTICS...
(In case you were wondering)

HOMEOWNERSHIP:

Top 3 states with the highest home ownership rate: West Virginia (77.6%), Delaware (76.8%) and Michigan (76.4%).

Top 3 states with the lowest home ownership rate: District of Columbia (47.2%), New York (55.9%) and California (58.3%).

67.8% of people own homes. (Unfortunately, they are not all owned free and clear) Source: Realtor.org

A home owner has a net worth approximately $30,000 higher than a renter.

The Federal Reserve reported that among household owners between the ages of 65 to 74 years old, household indebtedness continues to rise.

Source: US Census Bureau Report by: Kathleen Short and Amy O'Hara Housing and Household Economic Statistics Division

FORECLOSURE STATISTICS:

Foreclosure filings have exceeded 300,000 per month for the last 17 months. Source: CNBC.com

1 out of every 200 homes will be foreclosed upon. Source: Mortgage Bankers Association.

Every three months, 250,000 new families enter into foreclosure.   Source: FDIC.gov   Mortgage   Bankers Association.

TIPS FOR POTENTIAL HOME BUYERS AND MORTGAGE SEEKERS

1. **Buy a home within your means.** Just because you qualify for a larger home does not mean you should purchase one. Larger homes cost more to maintain and will deplete your net worth.

2. **Ensure your note rate is fixed.** An arm program is a mortgage where the interest rate periodically adjusts. Many lenders try to lure potential home buyers into these programs by offering lower rates than the standard fixed rate programs. However, when these rates adjust it is not uncommon that the first adjustment is over 2%! This makes a significant difference in your mortgage payment. For example, a $250k loan amortized over a 30 year period at 6% has a monthly principle and interest payment of $1,498. Based on the same scenario with a note rate of 8%, the payment jumps up to $1,834 per month. The difference? $336 per month! If you were to apply this difference on a monthly basis to the original note rate at 6%, you would shave off close to 10 years of mortgage payments!!! Total Savings: TENS of THOUSANDS of dollars. If you were to take that same $334 and invested it for 30 years,

at a 10% rate of return that money would grow to over $755,000! The bottom line? Fixed rates are the only way to go.

3. **Make sure you escrow your property taxes and insurance**. Waiving this option typically results in a higher interest rate which means less money in your pocket to apply towards building wealth. In addition to higher interest rates, you will have to come up with the full dollar amount when these bills come due. Unfortunately, most people do not set money aside to pay for these expenses and use credit to cover these costs. How costly could this be? It all depends on the interest being charged by your credit card provider. For example, let us assume your tax and insurance obligation is $2500 and the interest rate on the account used to cover this expense is 14.99%. Based on a 3% balance payment schedule, your monthly minimum payment required by the lending institution would be approximately $75 per month. If you did not accelerate the debt payoff and only made the minimum payments, this $2500 debt would cost you $3264. The total drain on your net worth? Over $760! Not only do you still have your normal principle and interest payments to make on a monthly basis, but now you have the added debt and burden of trying to pay off your back property taxes and insurance while simultaneously trying to save over $200 per month to cover next year's obligation.

4. **Take out a 30 year note.** I call this the safety factor. Most people realize if they do not consistently pay down the principle balance of their mortgage the interest paid over a full 30 year period would be staggering. A $250,000 loan at 6% would have an interest charge exceeding $289,000 based on a 30 year note! This is more than what you originally owed on the property. However, emergencies can and do arise and this is the reason I suggest you do a 30 year mortgage. If you were to take out a 15 or 20 year mortgage note, your monthly obligation would be substantially higher causing a financial hardship when emergencies surface. Granted the interest rates at shorter terms are typically 1/8% lower, but in my opinion the peace of mind that comes with the lower payment requirement outweighs the amount of extra interest paid. Besides, you will accelerate this debt payoff by following The Toxic Debt Solution™.

5. **Set up a bi-weekly payment plan.** This act alone will save you several year's worth of payments on a 30 year note. With a bi-weekly payment plan, you split your monthly payment in half. For example, if your current mortgage obligation is $1,000 per month, you would pay $500 every other week to your lender. Not all mortgage providers are going to offer this payment option in-house. If this is the case with the lender servicing your mortgage note, check with third party organizations like Paymap. For a small

monthly fee, they can coordinate this payment option for you.

6. **Do not use your equity.** You must view the equity in your home as part of your retirement plan. People who use the equity in their home will only delay becoming debt free and increase the cost of the home.
7. **Stop refinancing.** Data supports the average homeowner moves or refinances their home every 5-7 years. Constant refinancing only prolongs paying it off and can add years worth of payments back onto the note.

ANSWERS TO LIFE'S QUESTIONS: FOR POTENTIAL BUYERS

I CURRENTLY RENT, DOES IT REALLY MAKE FINANCIAL SENSE TO OWN A HOME? YES

Your net worth (The difference between your assets verses your liabilities) is the leading indicator of your ability to meet your financial goals and objectives. Statistics prove the net worth of a home owner is greater than the net worth of a non home owner. The figures vary depending upon the resource used, but it is safe to assume a home owner is worth about $30,000 more. There are a couple of reasons behind the numbers. A home is a forced savings plan. Every single month part of your mortgage obligation gets applied to the principle balance owed increasing your ownership in the property and your worth. Secondly, properties have a history of appreciation. Granted this might not hold true during recessionary times when the economy slows down and values decline, however a home is a long term investment and should be viewed as such. Let's assume you purchase a property for $200,000 in an area that has an average annual equity growth rate of 5%. After a 10 year period, the value on this property would exceed $325,000! Based on this scenario, owning a home would be like getting a $12,500 annual raise. However, before you make this transition, you need to be debt free, save up a 5% down payment and have between $1k- $3k in an emergency fund. This would ensure you do not stretch yourself too thin financially which only causes stress and disharmony in your life.

I NEED TO BUY A HOME, WHO SHOULD I USE?

Use a professional. Purchasing a property is one of the largest financial transactions you will possibly make. A **Realtor®** is an industry expert and will ensure you avoid many potential hazards that could be devastating to your financial well being. They will also keep you informed on all the details of the transaction so you and your family are protected. The National Association of Realtors has a membership base that exceeds 1.2 million. Each of these licensed professionals is subject to continuing education requirements and very knowledgeable.

SHOULD I HAVE A HOME WARRANTY POLICY? YES

If you are purchasing a home, make sure you ask the seller to pay for a home warranty. This fee will be a one-time charge paid at the time of the sellers closing and normally provides you and your family with coverage for 1 year. Having a policy in place will protect you against the high costs associated with repair or replacement of covered items. What is covered under a standard policy is going to vary by the insurance provider. Most policies cover general appliances, heating systems, water heater, plumbing and some electrical issues. Supplemental policy coverage could include a hot tub, washer/dryer and air conditioning units. If you are covered and have a problem, dial into the insurance company's service center and for a small fee, (Normally around $50) they will send a technician to repair or replace the problem item potentially saving you hundreds, if not thousands of dollars.

SHOULD I BUY A HOME WHILE I'M STILL IN DEBT?

Your primary focus should be on debt elimination. If you purchase a property while still in debt, the added expenses of home ownership would only chip away at your ability to break the chains of debt slavery and prolong the process of debt freedom. Let's assume you owed $25k worth of debt with an average interest rate of 12% (Quite low based on today's standards) and required by the lender to make a 2% minimum payment based off the monthly balance until the debt it paid. Keeping it simple, this would equal $500 per month. Based on these numbers and sticking to the $500 payment, it would take 72 months to get out of debt completely. If you factored in $400 extra you might be required to pay on a monthly basis as a home owner and applied that toward The Toxic Debt Solution™ as well, you would be out of debt within 32 months! Other reasons why you should wait until you are debt free before purchasing a home?

1. Paying off your obligations will increase your credit rating. (FICO Score) The higher your credit rating, the better the lending programs and associated interest rates. Talk about a windfall! This alone could save thousands of dollars in interest!

2. You would enter into home ownership with no other debt obligation. Less debt equals less stress. Do you really want to diminish your quality of life by taking on added obligations?

3. Not having debt obligations will allow you to save money for a down payment faster. A larger down payment will not only keep your payments low and save you money on interest, but possibly save you additional money by minimizing or totally eliminating the need for mortgage insurance.

WHAT TYPE OF DOWN PAYMENT IS REQUIRED TO PURCHASE AN OWNER OCCUPIED PROPERTY? DEPENDS

Down payment requirements vary depending upon the lending program and property type. Conventional lending down payment guidelines for single family residence is currently 5%. FHA lending programs have a 3 ½% down payment requirement. Some specialized loan programs like Rural Housing or a VA loan might not even require a down payment. I suggest you speak with a lending professional to obtain information on program guidelines and associated down payment requirements based on your situation.

DOES IT MATTER WHERE I GET MY MORTGAGE FROM? NO

It does not matter which mortgage company provides the funding to close your transaction. What matters is taking the time necessary to shop around and find the lowest interest rate and costs available. I suggest you speak with 3 separate mortgage providers and compare the difference. Go with the provider that offers you the best interest rate, note terms and closing costs. It is well worth the time and effort it takes to shop for a mortgage. Remember, even a slightly higher interest rate could mean tens of thousands of dollars in lost money.

WILL SHOPPING FOR A MORTGAGE IMPACT MY FICO SCORE/CREDIT RATING?

Fair Isaac was founded in 1956 by engineer Bill Fair and mathematician Earl Isaac. They developed the model that allows lenders and other creditors to assess the credit risk of a potential borrower. Having multiple lenders check your credit rating will impact your FICO score however, the impact is minimal unless you do not limit the amount of lenders that access your records. I suggest you limit your search to three separate providers. Each will check your credit history as reported by the three major credit bureaus. Each check will remain on your credit report as an inquiry for a 2 year period.

ANSWERS TO LIFE'S QUESTIONS: FOR EXISTING HOME OWNERS

SHOULD I HAVE A HOME WARRANTY IF I ALREADY OWN A HOME? DEPENDS

If you already own a home, it might not make financial sense to pay for a home warranty if the home is new or in relatively good condition. Why incur an additional expense? Odds are in your favor that this type of property will have minimum repair issues. In the event you are living in a home that is dated, then it might make financial sense. Evaluate your individual situation and make a healthy financial decision you feel comfortable with.

DOES IT MAKE SENSE TO PULL EQUITY OUT OF MY HOME AND DO A DEBT CONSOLIDATION? NO

Keep your equity in-tact. I have seen too many people fall into this trap only to rack up their credit card debt after the consolidation. The possible lower payment might be an initial draw, but once you take into consideration the cost of the transaction and the additional interest payments you would make since the debts would be amortized over the term of the note, most of the time it will not make financial sense. The best solution is to stop using credit and operate on a cash basis. Pay down your existing accounts using The Toxic Debt Solution™.

I NEED TO SELL A HOME, WHO SHOULD I USE?

Use a professional. A Realtor® is an industry expert that is licensed and has the ability to assess the current market value of your property. This is done by using the most recent and reliable information available. In addition to the market value, they will put together a marketing plan to maximize exposure of your property to potential buyers and handle the legal paperwork required for a smooth transaction. The National Association of Realtors has a membership base that exceeds 1 million people. Each of these professionals are licensed and subject to continuing education requirements as determined by the Division of Real Estate. This makes them the most suitable candidate for the job.

DO I HAVE TO PAY CAPITAL GAINS IF I SOLD MY HOME FOR A PROFIT? DEPENDS

According to the most recent IRS guidelines, if you have a home and used it as your primary residence for 2 out of the last 5 years, the first $250,000 in gains from the sale of the property is tax free. If you are married and the property is held jointly, your spouse could claim another $250,000 worth of tax free gains for a total of $500,000! This could save quite a bit of money since capital gains tax could be as much as 35%. Since IRS guidelines are subject to change, visit them at www.irs.gov for the most recent information.

IF I HAVE LOTS OF DEBT AND OWN A HOME, IS IT EVER OKAY TO SELL AND RENT? YES

If you are riding the wave of a financial tsunami, and wonder if it makes financial sense to rent verses keeping up with your mortgage obligations and the other expenses associated with home ownership, the answer is YES! Making the transition into a rental has the possibility of freeing up hundreds of dollars on a monthly basis. Not to mention if you are fortunate enough to sell your home for a profit, this extra money could be applied towards your debts and help get you planted on solid ground. If you desire to make this move, you must have a plan. Calculate the potential amount of money this type of transition would free up. Once the transaction is final, make a commitment to use this dollar amount to pay toward your debt obligations. Focus on becoming totally debt free before you transition back into home ownership.

CAN I SELL MY HOME IF I OWE MORE THAN WHAT IT IS WORTH? YES

A short sale is when you coordinate to sell your property for less than what you owe the bank. This type of transactions is subject to your lenders approval and could take several months to complete. To start the process, hire a professional Realtor. When interviewing agents, make sure you ask them about their experience in this area. Do not hire someone that is not experienced. A short sale is a difficult transaction to coordinate and not for the beginner. It is also important to note a lender could hold you legally responsible for the difference of what you owed verses what it sold for.

ARE THERE TAX IMPLICATIONS DUE TO A SHORT SALE? YES

The portion of the liability the lender was "Short" can be written off as a bad debt when reporting to the IRS. When this is done, you will receive a 1099-C Cancellation of Debt Form. You must claim this as income on your tax returns unless you can prove you were insolvent or the debt was included in a bankruptcy.

WILL A SHORT SALE IMPACT MY FICO SCORE? YES

Once the transaction closes and you sell the property, this account on your credit report will generally reflect a "settled" status. This description is an indication the lender did not receive what was originally owed to them which has a negative impact on your credit scoring. This designation will stay on your report for a 7 year period. However, it will have little impact on your scoring as time passes and you demonstrate a history of fiscal responsibility by paying your bills on time as required by your lenders.

ANSWERS TO LIFE'S QUESTIONS: FOR HOME OWNERS THAT CAN NO LONGER AFFORD THEIR MORTGAGE

IS THERE HOPE IF I'M FALLING BEHIND ON MY MORTGAGE PAYMENTS? YES

If you are not able to make your mortgage payments due to financial hardship, then coordinate with your lender and try to modify the terms of your loan. A loan modification is only a temporary fix to your problem since most interest rate/payment adjustments typically last no longer than a couple of years. If your financial issues are not short term, then sell your house. DO NOT WAIT. Try to sell the property even if current market conditions are not desirable. Contact a professional Realtor today and get the expertise and exposure required for a quicker sale. If the property is not worth the amount owed, coordinate through your agent to do a short sale on the property. Since shelter is a basic need, foreclosure should be your last option. Stop making payments on all of your other debts before you decide to stop paying a mortgage obligation.

CAN I COORDINATE WITH MY MORTAGE PROVIDER TO LOWER MY INTEREST RATE? MAYBE

Most lending organizations have a Financial Hardship Department designed to assist you. Every lender is quite unique in the type of help they are willing to offer. Most will start the process by sending you a kit of information by mail which will include a financial worksheet. Inside the packet, you will find detailed instructions on what the lender requires to evaluate your current financial situation. Be prepared to fill out ALL your debt obligations and living expenses on the worksheet. Ensure the worksheet includes all your expenses including: food, fuel, utilities, alimony, child support, insurance, childcare, dry cleaning, and any other expense specific to your family. Remember, not providing an accurate accounting of your expenditures will paint a flawed financial picture for the lender and they might decline your request for a loan modification not realizing you had other debt obligations you failed to include on your worksheet.

In addition to the worksheet, most lenders will require proof of assets and income. They usually request your recent bank and investment statements along with copies of your paystubs and tax documentation. Many will even request a letter of explanation highlighting the cause of your hardship. Based on this data, a representative will evaluate your financial situation to see if a modification is warranted. Please note there are no set guidelines a lender must follow. Loan modifications are solely left up to the lenders discretion.

Response timeframes for loan modification vary by lender and could take up to 3 months to process. They will contact you if it is determined you are eligible for assistance or send out notification by mail. Some of the more common modifications include:

- Lower interest rates.
- Changing your adjustable rate mortgage to a fixed rate for a specified period of time. Usually between 2-3 years.
- Waiving late payment or other fees charged.
- Keeping your interest rate, but lowering the payment for a certain period of time. Be VERY careful of this option. If the new payment does not cover the interest due based on your existing note,

the lender might add the difference to the principle balance owed!

- Waiving past due payments.

Since all modifications vary, ask your lender for specific details before initiating the process. If the solution they offer is not going to assist you financially, then why go through the process. Either way, it won't hurt to make the call.

I'M BEHIND ON MY MORTGAGE PAYMENTS AND THE LENDER OFFERED ME A DEED IN LIEU OF FORECLOSRE. WHAT IS THAT?

In most states, your name is on the title to your home. This means you own the property on record even if you have a mortgage. At your initial closing, you agreed to allow the lender to place a lien against the property for the amount you borrowed. A deed in lieu of foreclosure is a process of signing the property over to the lender and removing your name from title. This process is faster than coordinating a foreclosure through the court system and would allow the lender to move forward to liquidate the asset faster. If the sale of the home does not satisfy all the money you owed on a property including administrative fees and the cost of disposition, the lender has a legal right to sue you for the difference owed. However, this is rare.

DOES A DEED IN LIEU OF FORECLOSRE IMPACT MY CREDIT RATING? YES

A lender coordinates this process as a result of default. Any form of default reflected on your credit report has a negative impact on your credit rating and will stay on your report for a 7 year period.

I CAN NO LONGER AFFORD MY HOME, WHAT IS THE FORECLOSURE PROCESS?

The foreclosure process is initiated when you stop making your mortgage payments. Once your mortgage payment is not made and attempts to recover the funds are not successful, a lender files a Notice of Default or Lis Pendens at the County Recorder's Office. Doing this puts the borrower on notice they are facing foreclosure. The borrower then has a reinstatement period to bring their account current in order to avoid a foreclosure. If the account is delinquent after this time period lapses, (Usually 3 months) the borrower will receive a Notice of Sale. This notice will advise the borrower on the details of the pending sale including the time and location. This notice is also filed at the county and posted in the local newspaper. It is safe to assume the process normally takes a few months to finalize. State laws do vary and might include both judicial and non judicial foreclosures.

AM I RESPONSIBLE FOR TAXES IF THE LENDER WRITES OFF OR CANCELS MY DEBT OBLIGATION UPON FORECLOSURE OR MORTGAGE RESTRUCTING? YES, BUT...

If you owe a creditor and they cancel or forgive a debt, you are generally responsible for paying taxes on the amount forgiven. However, there are exceptions to this rule. The Mortgage Forgiveness Debt Relief Act of 2007 stipulates you will be excluded from the tax obligation on debt forgiven on a primary home through 2012. You will also be excluded for tax liability resulting from income derived from mortgage restructuring. Since legalities always change, consult the IRS for the most recent data.

HOW DOES A FORECLOSURE IMPACT MY FICO SCORE (CREDIT RATING)?

A foreclosure will be reflected on your credit report for a 7 year period and damages your credit score substantially; however your credit rating can be rebuilt.

I HAD A FORECLOSURE, HOW LONG DO I HAVE TO WAIT UNTIL I QUALIFY FOR ANOTHER HOME PURCHASE? 3 YEARS

According to Fannie Mae and Freddie Mac guidelines, the current waiting period is 3 years. This 3 year period starts from the date the foreclosure was finalized through the court system. It is not based off the initial filing date by the lender. This information will show up on your credit report for a 7 year period after the information is reported to the credit bureaus. During this waiting period, commit to becoming financially healthy by accomplishing the following:

1) Build up a $1-3k emergency fund
2) Pay off all delinquent accounts
3) Start a savings plan to build up enough money to cover the down payment required to purchase a new property

Do not worry if it takes you over 3 years to obtain the objectives stated above. Once they have been accomplished, you can move forward with a home purchase debt free and financially fit.

ANSWERS TO LIFE'S QUESTIONS: FOR INVESTORS

CAN I USE THE EQUITY IN MY HOME TO PURCHASE AN INVESTMENT PROPERTY? YES – (But only if it makes financial sense once you crunch the numbers)

Once you are debt free, focusing on building a 6 month emergency fund before you use the equity in your home to purchase an investment property. You must also crunch the numbers to ensure you are making a financially sound decision. First, a couple of rules, if you are going to take out an equity line of credit, ensure it has a fixed rate. You never want to place yourself in a situation where lenders can raise your payments by increasing your interest rate. Also, you only want to open the equity line up to the dollar amount you need to make the deal work and not a penny more. What is the reasoning behind this logic? If you have an open line available to you it might be used for other purposes outside of purchasing a property and get yourself into debt. Another reason is the new lender is going to include your monthly obligation on this note when determining your debt to income ratio. (The debt to income ratio or D.T.I. is determined by dividing the sum total of all your monthly debt obligations by your average monthly gross income) This ratio is one of the key factors a lender uses when trying to determine your credit worthiness and risk. If this ratio is too high, you could be declined for a loan. Currently, conforming guidelines have this ratio set at 38%. Exceeding this percentage means you are an increased risk and might not receive the financing you desire. However, with excellent credit and a strong asset profile, I have seen people secure financing with ratios in the 40 plus D.T.I. range.

WHAT ARE SOME OF THE THINGS I NEED TO CONSIDER WHEN CRUNCHING THE NUMBERS TO SEE IF AN INVESTMENT PROPERTY MAKES FINANCIAL SENSE?

This depends on the property objectives you have. If your goal is to play the role of a landlord and hold onto the property, rents received should be greater than the mortgage obligation and costs associated with property ownership. Some of the property costs would include: Mortgage obligations, (Inclusive of an equity line if one was used for down payment purposes) property taxes, hazard insurance, snow removal, garbage disposal, lawn care, general maintenance and utility payments. Other obligations you must factor into the equation that are not as obvious should include:

- The costs associated with securing a renter. This could be done by using a property management company. Fees vary, but could equal one month's rent.
- The cost of getting the property rental ready. (New paint, flooring, doors, windows, or other expenses) Not only do you need to factor in the cost of supplies, but also the contractor fees in the event you are not a handyman.

- The average vacancy rate for your area. Always play it safe. Chances are very high you will not have a renter every month of the year.

DO I HAVE TO PAY CAPITAL GAINS TAX IF I SOLD MY INVESTMENT PROPERTY FOR A PROFIT? YES

You are responsible for paying capital gains tax on any profit received from the sale of an investment property. To delay this tax obligation, investors can use a 1031 exchange. A 1031 exchange allows real estate investors to use the gains received from the sale of a property towards the purchase of a new investment property.

TIPS FOR A MORE REWARDING AND FULFILLING LIFE

BE POSITIVE

"As ye sow, so shall ye reap." Some might call this principle the Law of Attraction, others might consider it karma. Whatever you prefer to consider it, like attracts like. Most people do not attract negativity unless they are negative. If you ever wonder why your life is full of negativity, start doing a little soul searching. Chances are very high your underlying thought patterns have not been positive. Being negative is not constructive when trying to achieve a happy and healthy state of living. Every time you catch yourself reacting to a stressful situation in a negative way, smile! Consciously decide to make the change and alter your reaction to the situation. Look at it as a learning opportunity for your personal development and growth. Remember, you choose how to react in every situation you are faced with. The choice is yours. Nobody has control over your emotions. Nobody can make you mad, angry or sad. On the other hand, nobody can make you happy, content or at peace. Remember, the choice is yours. Choose to be happy!

RESOURCES TO CONSIDER

www.Realtor.org - This site currently hosts millions of homes for sale and homes for rent. Not only can you search for properties throughout the United States using a variety of criteria, you can also seek the professional service and knowledge only a licensed Realtor can offer.

www.City-Data.com - When you are ready to jump into the market as a potential home buyer, do your homework. Know the details of the city or town you are thinking about buying a property in. This website is full of wonderful information including estimated home values, population, median household income and median population age.

IRS: 1-800-829-1040 - It's exciting to make a profit on investment properties, until the capital gains tax comes due. Worried about the tax implications of selling a property, speak to your C.P.A. or an IRS professional.

www.tenant-screeing.com or www.aTenantScreen.com - In the market for a tenant? Then why not save money and do the background check yourself. These sites allow you to verify or check a potential tenant's employment, credit and possible criminal history.

www.biggerpockets.com /foreclosurelaw - This website provides a synopsis of foreclosure laws by state.

www.nationwidehomewarranty.com - This organization offers home warranty options to ensure you are protected.

CORE PRINCIPLE 7

INSURANCE: BORING YET CRITICAL

Heath care costs continue to skyrocket. Being diagnosed with an unexpected illness could cost you hundreds of thousands of dollars in diagnostic and treatment care. If your family is dependent upon you for their financial well being, an untimely death will cause a financial hardship and might result in the loss of your home and other assets. In addition to possible health issues, natural disasters continue to cause billions of dollars in property damage every year. The risk associated with not being properly insured is great. Insurance is a safeguard and gives you peace of mind. It is designed to protect you and your loves ones from financial ruin. This safeguard is a must and will help keep your estate and assets protected. It is not a matter of "If" you will ever need insurance; it's a matter of when!

INTERESTING STATISTICS...
(In case you were wondering)

How many people live without health insurance?

1 in 5 adults in the United States does not have health insurance. Stats provided by: Center for Disease Control

What are my chances of suffering a life changing disability?

- 3 in 10 people that enter the workforce today will become disabled before retiring

- 1 in 7 workers can expect to be disabled for five years or more before retirement
- Over 51 Million Americans are classified as disabled, representing 18% of the population
- In the U.S., a disabling injury occurs every 1 second. A fatal injury occurs every 4 minutes

Stats provided by: The Council for Disability Awareness: www.disabilitycanhappen.org

How many people do not carry life insurance?

Studies show that 40% of adult Americans have no life insurance whatsoever and over 50 million people in this country lack adequate coverage.

> Source: Too Many People Lack Adequate Life Insurance Coverage. Article posted by JDPower.com

What is the average life expectancy?

According to the CDC National Center for Health Statistics, the average life expectancy is 78 years.

ANSWERS TO LIFE'S QUESTIONS

SHOULD I HAVE A LIFE INSURANCE POLICY? DEPENDS

Life insurance is designed to protect your loved ones who are dependent upon you financially. If you are not married and do not have dependents, I do not suggest you carry a policy unless you do not have the money to cover the cost of your funeral. In this case, I suggest a small term policy up to $15k. If you are a W-2 waged employee, check with your employer. They might already have a small policy in place as an additional benefit to cover these expenses.

HOW MUCH LIFE INSURANCE SHOULD I CARRY? 10X's YOUR ANNUAL SALARY

The purpose of life insurance is to protect your loved ones who are dependent upon you financially. You should have enough insurance to replace your annual salary if the money was invested at an annual rate of return of 10%. For example, if you earn $45,000 annually you should have a $450,000 life insurance policy. ($450,000 X 10% = $45,000)

WHAT TYPE OF INSURANCE SHOULD I GET? MOST PEOPLE SHOULD GET TERM INSURANCE

There are two main umbrellas of insurance. The first is called Term and the other is called Permanent Life. Term is easy to acquire and pays a death benefit to your beneficiary. It does not build up a cash value like permanent insurance so your premiums will be lower. Lower premiums will free up additional money to apply towards The Toxic Debt Solution™.

SHOULD I CARRY A RENTER'S POLICY IF I DO NOT OWN A HOME? YES

The average renter has between $15k-$20k worth of assets in their home. This figure would include furniture, jewelry, clothes, computers, electronics and other household goods. My suggestion is to carry enough renters insurance to cover your loss in the event a fire or other disaster destroys all your possessions. It is also important to know this type of policy might limit your claim for jewelry theft. Speak to an agent at a reputable provider and get all the details. To prove your claim, keep documented records of purchases and appraisals. Also develop a list of items you have in your home. If you have collectibles, art work or expensive jewelry, an appraisal would ensure you get the maximum value. I also suggest videotaping your possessions as added proof, you have them. Doing this would make processing a claim much easier. It is important to note this type of policy will not cover damages resulting from floods. If you are residing in a flood zone, you need to carry a separate policy to be covered. Since floods are one of the more common hazards, I highly recommend this type of a policy. All flood insurance is underwritten though the federal government. However, any broker can draft up the policy details. Not sure if your residence is in a Flood Zone? Then access www.freeflood.com. This site will provide you with a risk factor based on your property address. Anything above a low rating should indicate a possible need for this form of insurance. For a couple of dollars, FEMA has a map search option that can be queried using your property address. (www.fema.gov) Like any insurance policy, the higher the deductable, the lower the premiums. Pick a premium level you feel comfortable with.

I RENT A PORTION OF A HOME. AM I PROTECTED UNDER MY LANDLORD'S HOME

OWNERS INSURANCE POLICY IN CASE SOMETHING HAPPENS? NO

A home owner's policy protects the assets of the owner not the renter. If you want protection, you need to take out a renter's policy.

I OWN A CONDO OR TOWNHOME; DO I NEED INSURANCE FOR MY PROPERTY? YES

Most people that own these types of residences are under the impression they are covered under the blanketed insurance policy the Home Owners Association carries for the development, however they are mistaken! This type of insurance only covers the losses associated with damage done to the exterior of your unit. In other words, the building itself is covered, your possessions are not. If you are this type of homeowner, I suggest you obtain a renter's policy for your protection.

SHOULD I PAY TO INSURE MY APPLIANCES OR ELECTRONICS AT THE TIME OF PURCHASE? NO

Most new appliances and electronics already come with a manufactures warranty. Usually this type of protection covers you due to product malfunction and manufacturing defects. It normally does not cover damage resulting from accidents or water damage. So take good care of your purchases. Many companies try to lure you into purchasing of an extended warranty or a supplemental policy, but it comes at a cost and most of the time is not used.

SHOULD I HAVE DISABILITY INSURANCE? YES

This form of insurance provides a safety net by paying you an income benefit if a disability prevents you from working. Think of the financial stress you would be under if a disability prevented you from earning a paycheck. The consequences would be disastrous! If you are a W-2 waged employee, your employer might offer this insurance as a benefit. However, most employers view this type of insurance as a supplemental policy their employees have to pay for. Either way, find out if it is available for you. The typical policy will provide you with up to 60% of your income due to a disability. There are generally two policy types. The first pays a benefit if you are not able to do the work you are currently engaged in. The other policy only pays if your disability prevents you from working at all. Touch base with a couple of different providers and review your options.

IF I AM HEALTHY, SHOULD I DROP MY HEALTH INSURANCE TO SAVE MONEY? NO

Insurance is critical to have. Even if you are healthy, you are not immune to accidents. Statistics vary, but it is safe to assume there are millions of vehicle accidents alone costing billions of dollars annually in medical care. This does not take into consideration the risk of being involved in a work related mishap or other unforeseen disasters. Health insurance will ensure you and your family are protected. Need affordable health insurance?

Access www.ehealthinsurance.com. This site will provide you with health insurance quotes from leading providers within the industry.

WHAT ARE MY HEALTH INSURANCE OPTIONS IF I RECENTLY LOST MY JOB?

Start your search for affordable health insurance immediately. www.eheathinsurance.com is a great place to begin. COBRA also provides temporary continuation of heath care benefits at group rates which could possibly save you money. Benefit eligibility varies depending upon the reason that caused you to lose your benefits to begin with. One specific event could include voluntary or involuntary termination of employment. For a list of qualified events or for other detailed information regarding this type of insurance option, contact the United Sates Department of Labor at: www.dol.gov

DO I NEED LONG TERM CARE INSURANCE? YES

Everyone is going to reach a stage in their lives where Long Term Care Insurance (LTCI) is going to be needed. LTCI offers coverage and protection for individuals that require nursing home or assisted living facility care. According to an article posted by New York Life, the cost of this type of care increases on an annual basis. Fees for a private room could range from $80,000 to over $125,000 per year! There are different variables that determine monthly premiums. The first is your age. The older you are the more expensive a policy will be. Next, is the type of items the plan will cover. Like any type of insurance, the greater the coverage, the higher the premiums. Finally, the state of your health is the last factor. Many providers will not insure people with pre-existing conditions because they pose a greater risk of using policy benefits. LTCI benefits and eligibility requirements vary greatly by provider. My suggestion is to get a policy when you are between the ages of 55-60. However, when it comes to insurance, do what makes you feel comfortable in order to protect yourself and your loves ones.

RESOURCES TO CONSIDER

Insurance Providers:

Aflac - www.aflec.com   1-800-992-3522

MetLife - www.metlife.com

Nationwide - www.nationwide.com or 1-877-669-6877

Liberty Mutual - www.libertymutal.com or 888-333-8389

TIPS FOR A MORE REWARDING AND FULFILLING LIFE

EXPRESS GRADITUDE

Gratitude is one of the most noble of virtues. Always recognize the blessings in your life. Do not place blame on any other person for your financial situation or any other aspect of your personal life. You must realize that you are the master of your own destiny and responsible for creating your own happiness. If you are seeking abundance, how could you expect God to bless you with increased measure if you do not express gratitude for what you already have? You must not only show gratitude for life changing events that occur, but also for the small day to day thoughtfulness of others. It could be expressed verbally by speaking kind words, or physically by offering a warm handshake, loving embrace or simply expressed with a smile or thank you note.

CORE PRINCIPLE 8

UNDERSTANDING THE WILD AND CRAZY WORLD OF PENSION FUNDS, 401Ks, SAVING ACCOUNTS AND OTHER INVESTMENT VEHICLES

This is one area of financial management most people neglect. This topic appears quite complex on the surface. You are faced with a variety of investment options to choose from. Stocks, bonds, mutual funds, treasury notes, commodities, precious metals... The list of options seems to be endless. Yes, on the surface investing appears to be a wild and crazy world, but even crazier is not having a plan and participating. Do what is necessary and seek the education required to make sound investment decisions. Invest in your future by wisely investing your money.

If you refuse and give up your right to invest, then you are choosing to give up your future. My heart aches every time I see a person in their "golden years" struggling to survive. If they are healthy enough, they are forced to continue working or they must rely upon the generosity of friends and family members for their survival. You do not have to search very far to find them in the workforce. They pack your groceries and hand out food samples at wholesale clubs. Some are cashiers, fast food cooks and others might be food and beverage servers. They usually work long hard hours standing on their feet only to be compensated minimum wage. Decide today this is NOT going to be your fate!

INTERESTING STATISTICS...
(In case you were wondering)

- According to the Center on Budget and Policy Priorities, excluding Social Security, nearly one out of every two elderly people has income levels below the poverty line.

- The average family saves less than 2% of their "net" income on an annual basis.

- According to data from the U.S. Census Bureau, the real median household income level is $52,029.

THINGS TO THINK ABOUT

- Based on the statistics above, the average family saves less than $1k annually!

- How much would the average monthly savings amount of $90 grow to if it was invested at an 8% rate of return until the retirement age of 65?

    25 Years Old = $314,190

    35 Years Old = $134,132

    45 Years Old = $53,013

    55 Years Old = $16,465

DO NOT WAIT! Get yourself out of debt and start saving for retirement A.S.A.P. The longer you wait, the less your investments will grow. Decide TODAY that you will not be dependent upon someone else financially when you retire.

- You would need over $703,000 to sustain yourself for 15 retirement years based on the real median household income level.
- Expenses for the elderly do not decrease with age. Factors that must be taken into consideration is the rising costs of health coverage, medication, long term care insurance, funeral planning and life insurance premium adjustments.

ANSWERS TO LIFE'S QUESTIONS

IS MY 401K PROTECTED IF MY COMPANY GOES BANKRUPT OR OUT OF BUSINESS? YES

Under Federal Law, retirement plan assets are kept in a trust account and not considered an asset of the company. Therefore your money is 100% safe and sound.

WHEN COMPLETING MY TAXES, I OWE MONEY. IS THERE ANYTHING I CAN DO TO LOWER MY TAX OBLIGATION BEFORE THE APRIL 15 DEADLINE? YES

A qualified retirement plan like an IRA can help lower your most recent year tax obligations. By contributing to a qualified plan like a Traditional IRA, you can deduct dollar for dollar against your taxable income. The lower the taxable income you claim, the less in taxes you will owe. To take advantage of this benefit, contributions must be made no later than April 15th. (The tax deadline) Contributions to a plan after this timeframe can only be used to offset the existing years' tax obligation. Of course, in order to take advantage of this you need to have the money for investment purposes. Do not use your Emergency Fund to cover this investment. You must also understand this investment is for retirement purposes and should be considered a long term investment. (10 years or greater) Should you liquidate the account before certain criteria is met (including age limitations) you would be subject to a penalty and tax.

I DECIDED TO LIQUIDATE MY RETIREMENT ACCOUNT, WHAT ARE SOME OF THE THINGS I SHOULD BE AWARE OF?

I'm all for keeping your retirement intact. However, if you choose to liquidate the account due to a medical or some other significant reason, make sure all the money is used wisely. Funds should not be used for any other purpose unless it is medically related. For tax deferred retirement accounts (IRAs, 401K, 403B) if you are withdrawing the money before the age of 59 ½, you will be subject to a 10% early withdrawal fee. You will also be responsible for the tax obligation on these funds the year the money was liquidated. Run the numbers and be cautious you do not place yourself in a higher tax bracket. Doing this will subject yourself to additional tax liability not only on the money being liquidated, but your entire income potentially costing you thousands of dollars more. There are certain reasons an early withdrawal can be made penalty fee. (Such as becoming disabled or due to financial hardship) Even then, certain guidelines must be met. Speak to the human resource advisor who is in charge of coordinating your company's retirement planning for the details.

SHOULD I START SAVING FOR MY CHILD'S EDUCATION WHILE I STILL HAVE DEBT? NO

The added burden of saving for a child's education while you still have debt obligations does not make financial sense. You need to be financially stable before offering assistance to loved ones. Remember, children have time on their side and you might not. You will be more of a burden on your children if you need to depend upon them for your financial stability in your golden years.

I CAN'T PAY MY DEBTS. CAN I USE MY CHILDRENS 529 ACCOUNT? YES... BUT

A 529 account allows you to set money aside for your children to assist them with paying the costs associated with obtaining a college education. (Tuition, room & board, fees, books and supplies) Money invested in this account is exempt from federal taxation. If the funds are liquidated and used for any other purpose, a 10% penalty will be assessed and the money will be categorized as income for tax purposes. It is important to note that you are in charge of fund disbursements until your child reaches the age of majority. (Usually ranges between 18-21 depending upon state law) At this time, the child becomes the custodian of the account. If you are struggling to pay your bills, you can liquidate your child's 529 account, but only after all other options have been exhausted including the possibility of getting a part time job to make up the short fall.

DOES IT MAKE FINANCIAL SENSE TO PARTICIPATE IN MY EMPLOYERS RETIREMENT PLAN WHILE I'M STILL IN DEBT? DEPENDS

I recommend you participate up to the employer match and not a dollar more. My reasoning? An employer match will provide an instant rate of return equal to the match. So if they contribute a 50% match, your instant return on investing is 50%! If the employer does not match, I recommend you run the numbers and do what makes financial sense. To do this properly, you must compare the potential Return on Investment (ROI) against the interest rates on your liabilities. If the interest received from investing is greater than the interest on your debt obligations, then it makes financial sense to invest. Most of the time if your employer does not currently offer a match plan, chances are high it will make more financial sense to apply the extra money toward your debt obligations. (Especially if you are making mortgage payment)

Not sure where to find a mutual funds average Return on Investment? www.morningstar.com Is a wonderful website full of financial news and information including year to date and historical return on investment.

WHAT IS THE MAXIMUM CONTRIBUTION I CAN MAKE TO AN IRA?

For a Traditional IRA, you can make an individual contribution up to $5,000 or 10% of your salary (whichever is less). For individuals that are 50 and above, contributions have a maximum limit of $6000. For future years, check with the IRS for changes in retirement plans including contribution guidelines and limitations.

I PARTICIPATE IN MY EMPLOYERS RETIREMENT PLAN; CAN I ALSO CONTRIBUTE TO AN IRA? YES

Participating in an employer's retirement plan does not mean you can't contribute to an IRA account.

CAN I CONTRIBUTE TO A ROTH IRA?

A ROTH IRA has income limitations. Participating in this retirement plan will depend on the amount of income you make. A single individual must make below $105,000 to participate at the plans maximum level. Between $105,000 -$120,000 allows you to participate based on a prorated contribution. If your income levels exceeding $120,000, then you would not be allowed to contribute to this plan.

For a married couple filing jointly, you must make below $166,000 to participate at the plans maximum level. If you earn $166,000 to $176,000 you are allowed to participate with a prorated contribution. If your income levels exceeding $176,000 you would not be allowed to contribute to this plan.

Currently, ROTH IRA contributions have a $5000 maximum limit. For those that are 50 and above, contributions have a maximum limit of $6000. For future years, check with the IRS for changes in contribution guidelines and investment limitations.

WHAT IS A 401K PLAN AND WHAT IS THE MAXIMUM AMOUNT I CAN CONTRIBUTE?

A 401K is a company sponsored retirement plan. Employees contribute into an investment account using tax deferred contributions. Some company sponsored plans offer provisions that allow the employer to match a certain percentage of the employee's contribution. This is what I call FREE MONEY! If you still have debt, try to participate up to the employer match. Currently, the maximum employee contribution to this plan can't exceed $16,500 or 10% of your gross income (Whichever is less). For people age 50 or above, based on employer guidelines, the IRS will also allow an additional contribution of $5,500. This contribution is known within the investment community as a "Catch Up" payment.

WHAT IS A 403B PLAN AND WHAT IS THE MAXIMUM AMOUNT I CAN CONTRIBUTE?

A 403B is a retirement plan offered to employees working for organizations that are tax-exempt such as churches, schools, hospitals or other charitable organizations. Just like a 401K, these plans offer employees the option to contribute tax deferred money into an account for retirement purposes. Contributions to these plans are based upon a percentage of your income and the number of years of service you have in the organization. Currently the maximum employee contribution for this plan can't exceed $16,500 or 10% of your monthly gross income (Whichever is less). For people age 50 or above the IRS will also allow an additional contribution of $5,500. This contribution is known within the investment community as a "Catch Up" payment.

IS MY PENSION PROTECTED IF MY EMPLOYER GOES OUT OF BUSINESS? MAYBE

If your employer offers a plan not insured under PBGC guidelines, it is not protected if the employer goes belly-up. The PBGC is a federal agency created by the Employee Retirement Income Security Act of 1974. (www.pbgc.gov) This organization insures defined benefit plans (a plan that pays a specified amount on a monthly basis) for millions of Americans. To find out if your pension is protected, ask your employer for a copy of the "Summary Plan Description." Pension plan benefits vary depending upon several factors including plan assets, your age and other provisions. Currently, the max guaranteed amount per month is $4500.

SHOULD I INVEST FIRST OR FOCUS ON GETTING OUT OF DEBT? GET OUT OF DEBT!

Your primary focus on the road that leads you toward financial success starts with debt freedom. Focus all of your energy and effort towards paying off your debt obligations before investing. (Unless your employer offers a match program as previously discussed) It is rare you could receive a greater rate of return on an investment verses paying off your mortgage obligation. Even if your mortgage rate is 5% and you could get a R.O.I. (Return on Investment) at a greater percentage, it will still make financial sense most of the time to pay off your mortgage. The reason is your mortgage is up front interest. Yes, your rate might be 5%, but this is the interest rate over a 30 year term. Chances are very high your calculated interest rate on a monthly basis is much higher. For example, lets' assume you have a $200,000 mortgage obligation. The details of the note are as follows: 5% interest rate paid over a 30 year term. (Not that you would ever want to take 30 years to pay off your property) Based on the above, your monthly principle and interest payments would be $1073. Close to 80% of this initial payment will get applied towards interest not the principle portion of your mortgage note. As a matter of fact, to hit the 50/50 mark, where 50% of your mortgage payment gets applied towards the principle balance owed and 50% goes towards the interest, you would have to make 16 years worth of payments! This being the case and the fact the average family moves every 5-7 years, people are paying mostly interest and lots of it.

To figure out your own calculation, take the interest paid during a particular month and divide it against the total principle and interest payment.

MY INVESTMENT ACCOUNTS HAVE GONE DOWN SIGNIFICANTLY, SHOULD I CUT MY LOSSES AND LIQUIDATE THE ACCOUNTS? NO

Mutual funds and stocks are long term investments and subject to market volatility. The key word here is long term investment (10 years or greater). When the market suffers a major downward shift, now is not the time to panic. A loss is not realized until your account is liquidated. Until then, it is only considered a paper loss. If your investments have a history of producing a fruitful return, when the market swings in an upward trend you will probably recover. (Not that past performance is always going to dictate future profitability) A couple of ways you can minimize risk is to ensure your portfolio is diversified. As the saying goes, never place all your eggs in one basket. You also want to make sure your money is reallocated into safer investment option the older you get. Safer investments are ones that limit your risk and preserve your liquidity. These investment options usually offer a lower rate of return. Remember, any stock based investment must be considered long term. Another way to limit your risk is through dollar cost averaging. This is when you invest a specific dollar amount on a regular basis. When the market is down, your portfolio is worth less. However, through dollar cost averaging, you are able to purchase more of the security during this time increasing the value of your portfolio faster once the market adjusts upward.

WHAT ARE MUTUAL FUNDS?

A mutual fund offers a diverse collection of stocks or bonds and sold to investors as shares. Each fund provides an investor with instant diversification which is one of the benefits of this investment type. All mutual funds are professionally managed which appeal to the novice investor. For additional knowledge about mutual funds, access www.investopedia.com.

HOW DO I KNOW THE MONEY IN MY BANK IS PROTECTED IN CASE OF LENDER FAILURE?

To safeguard your deposits, ensure your lender is FDIC (Federal Deposit Insurance Corporation) insured. The FDIC is an independent agency of the government originally created after the Great Depression due to the many bank failures through the 20s and early 30s. The FDIC preserves and promotes consumer confidence by insuring deposits in banks and thrift institutions. Amounts protected will vary by year. It is also important to know the FDIC does not insure securities, mutual funds or other type of investment accounts. For additional information or to find out if your bank is FDIC insured, access www.fdic.gov.

IF MY DEPOSITS AT A LENDING INSTITUTION EXCEED THE FDIC INSURED LIMMIT, WHAT SHOULD I DO?

Open an account with a different lender. This will diversify where your money is being held and lower the risks associated with lender default.

DOES THE FDIC PROTECT MY DEPOSITORY ACCOUNTS IN CREDIT UNIONS? NO... But

All federal credit unions and state credit unions that are federally insured offer protection. A list of federally insured credit unions can be accessed at http://www.ncua.gov NCUA stands for the National Credit Union Administration. This administration supervises and insures savings in federal and most state chartered credit unions through the National Credit

Union Share Insurance Fund. (NCUSIF) The NCUSIF is a federal fund insuring accounts up to at least $100,000. Just like the FDIC, it is backed by the "Full Faith and Credit" of the U.S. government. Make sure your money is safeguarded and only use credit unions that offer this protection.

HOW DO I KNOW MY INVESTMENT ACCOUNTS ARE PROTECTED IF MY BROKERAGE COMPANY FAILS?

The Securities Investor Protection Corporation (SIPC) is designed to protect investors from bankrupt or troubled brokerage firms. They offer protection of up to $500,000 of securities already registered in your name or in the process of being registered. This coverage limitation also includes a $100,000 maximum claim for cash. For additional information or to find out if your brokerage is an SIPC member, you can contact the SIPC's membership department at 202-371-8300 or access them online at www.sipc.org. It's important to note this organization does not protect investment losses associated with market volatility or investment fraud. Since guidelines and insured amounts are subject to change, always access the SIPC website for the most recent information.

WHAT CAN I DO TO MINIMIZE THE POSSIBILITY OF INVESTMENT FRAUD?

According to the Securities Investor Protection Corporation, investment fraud in the U.S. ranges between $10-40 Billion a year! I'm unaware of any insurance company or governmental agency that protects your investments from fraud. The best way to minimize your risk is through education and research. If you are using an investment advisor, take the time to do a background check. Did they certify as a financial planner? The Financial Planning Association can provide imperative information on a potential advisors background including: Their experience, areas of specialty, licenses, certification and affiliations. This site will also provide you insight on their fees and compensation charges. They can be accessed online at www.fpaforfinancialplanning.org. If you are in the process of hiring an advisor, get referrals and search for an advisor that has your best interest at heart. Interview them and ask how they are going to help you accomplish your financial objectives. A reputable financial advisor will develop a plan based on your needs and will always be proactive.

RESOURCES TO CONSIDER

morningstar.com - A site filled with financial news and information including sections relating to stocks, bonds, mutual funds, options, ETFs and hedge funds.

bankrate.com - A great site for product and rate comparison. It has informational areas dedicated toward CDs, checking, saving and college financing. The site also has a retirement planning calculator so you could determine the projected future value on your investment accounts.

investopedia.com - Investopedia is a Forbes Digital Company. This website is exceptionally informative and features articles, market statistics and analysis. It has sections to help the novice or seasoned investor learn more about retirement, personal finance, foreign exchange, options, futures and mutual funds.

www.fpaforfinancialplanning.org - Need help looking for a Financial Planner? This site is home to the Financial Planning Association. This association was developed on January 1st 2000 when the Institute of Certified Financial Planners and the International Association for Financial Planners joined forces.

pbgc.gov - PBGC is a federal corporation created by the Employee Retirement Income Security Act of 1974. It currently protects the pensions of nearly 44 million American workers and retirees in more than 29,000 private single-employer and multiemployer defined benefit pension plans.

sipc.org - The Securities Investor Protection Corporation has been safeguarding the assets of investors for decades. From its creation by congress in 1970, they made possible the recovery of over $16 Billion in assets that investors would have otherwise lost due to brokerage closure and other financial difficulties.

fdic.gov - The Federal Deposit Insurance Corporation has protected consumer deposits for over 75 years. This site has information regarding deposit insurance, consumer protection, industry analysis, related news, events and also features a consumer resource center.

ncua.gov - The National Credit Union Administration (NCUA) is a federal agency that charters and monitors federal credit unions and insures savings in federal and some state-chartered credit unions across the country. Access this site to ensure your deposits in credit unions are protected.

TIPS FOR A MORE REWARDING AND FULFILLING LIFE

BE CHARITABLE

Many of the world's most financially successful people are philanthropists. They always take time to give of their talents and money. On your journey towards success in life you must look for opportunities to serve humanity. The world is in desperate need of helping hands. According to the United States Department of Health and Human Services, the poverty guideline for an average family of five is $24,800 or below. This statistic tells us that there are millions of men, women and children living in poverty. Statistics also show people that live at or below poverty guidelines have a higher disposition towards illness and medical care. There are many ways you can give back. Search for an opportunity to serve. Donate your time and financial resources to a reputable charity or organization and enjoy the fruits of serving others. These fruits include an increased sense of self-worth, inner peace and happiness.

CORE PRINCIPLE 9

LOVE, MARRIAGE AND DEBT OBLIGATIONS

Oh, the happy young couple embarking on a new life's journey of love and marriage. Exciting? Yes! Challenging? Absolutely! If you want to have a more peaceful coexistence with your eternal companion, you must find ways to communicate in a constructive manner when it comes to family finances. You must be open and honest in all things, especially where money is concerned. I have witnessed many loving relationships that have turned sour due to financial mismanagement. The old saying "when bills come through the door, love flies out the window," holds true to many couples faced with today's financial burdens. Whether you are a newlywed or a seasoned veteran, married for many years, you must develop the skill-set required for a truly successful marriage. A marriage not only based on the principles of love, honesty, integrity and loyalty, but on mutual respect, communication and "Financial Fidelity". What is Financial Fidelity? To be faithful and strict in your observance and management of the financial affairs of your home.

INTERESTING STATISTICS...
(In case you were wondering)

A variety of sources indicate between 50-60% of all marriages fail. Money is cited as the number one reason for divorce followed by infidelity.

States with the highest divorce numbers include: Nevada, Arkansas, Florida, Texas and New York (Source: CDC)

TIPS ON HOW TO PROMOTE FINANCIAL FIDELITY

1. Do not hide purchases from your spouse. If you need to hide something, then chances are you should not be buying it in the first place. Remember, your ultimate responsibility is your family's welfare. Consistently making purchases that are not necessary is not the roadmap towards a healthy financial future.
2. Do not hide debt obligations from your spouse. Secretly racking up credit card or other debts could be devastating to your marriage.
3. Do not hide or keep secret accounts from your partner.
4. Set financial goals as a couple and actively participate in developing a budget.

5. Hold a monthly "Money Talk" with your spouse. Review the family budget and discuss areas that might require more discipline and management.

6. Set individual spending limits. Decide on a dollar amount each of you could spend on a weekly basis. Use the money on whatever you desire. Doing this will allow you to make purchases without the constant need of approval from your spouse.

7. One person should not carry the burden and be responsible for the financial management of the home. Take turns paying the bills and auditing your accounts. Better yet, do it together.

8. If you want to make an "unnecessary" purchase that was not budgeted or covered by your weekly allotment, first discuss it with your spouse.

9. Make a pact to operate exclusively on a cash basis. Getting further into debt does not lead to a healthy relationship.

10. Be honest and own up to your mistakes.

ANSWERS TO LIFE'S QUESTIONS

AM I RESPONSIBLE FOR MY SPOUSES DEBTS IF THEY ARE NOT IN MY NAME? MAYBE

The answer to this question depends on the state in which you reside so check your state law. In many states if the debt was incurred during your marriage, you would be responsible regardless if your name is on the debt or not. This practice is common for community property states. If the debt was incurred before your marriage, and your name is not added to the account, you will not be responsible. To find out if your state is a community property state, access www.wikipedia.org and do a search on "Community Property".

IF MY SPOUSE HAS DEBTS IN DEFAULT, SHALL WE KEEP JOINT ASSETS? NO

Creditors have a legal right to any asset your spouse has their name on including liquid accounts, property and investments. Since they could seek judgment through our court system to get paid, keep your accounts separate.

IF MY SPOUSE FILES FOR BANKRUPTCY WILL I BE RESPONSIBLE FOR THE DEBTS? MAYBE

Having a Federal Court judge dismiss the obligation from your spouse does not offer you any protection. If your name is on the account or the debt was incurred during your marriage you might be responsible for full payment. However, you will not be responsible for any debt obligation incurred before the marriage.

AM I RESPONSIBLE FOR DEBTS ACCUMULATED DURING MY MARRIAGE IF THE DIVORCE DECREE SAYS I'M NOT? YES

When going through a divorce, it does not matter who the judge states is responsible for the payment of your obligations. If you co-borrowed or co-signed with or for your ex, you are responsible for payment to the lender in eyes of the law. Showing the creditor your divorce documentation as proof you are no longer responsible for payment means nothing. You signed the initial note, promise to pay or credit application which means you are the responsible party. If payments are not made, your credit will be impacted and suffer the negative consequences of default.

TIPS FOR A MORE REWARDING AND FULFILLING LIFE

BE A MAN OR WOMAN OF PROMISE

While I was a poor struggling college student, I was fortunate enough to obtain summer employment working for a clothing distribution Company. During those months I worked exceptionally hard in their Customer Service Department, specifically in an area called Returns. This area had a small handful of other employees, and we were responsible for the coordination of all product returns usually resulting from a wrong product shipment or defect. Two or three weeks into my employment I realized this area of the company lacked organization and my fellow co-workers were not applying themselves to take care of our customers in a timely fashion. I guess I was not the only one that realized the havoc of the division, our very outspoken manager, Rose, ripped through that department with a quick restructure. When she was finished, the only people that remained standing was a very pregnant supervisor named Cheryl and me. Within a month Cheryl left to deliver her child which left me by myself for most of the summer. Before I left the company, all the backlogged paperwork I found on my old colleagues desks were current and our customers were once again satisfied versus frustrated and on the verge of cancelling their relationship with the company. Two weeks before school started, I trained a couple of new staff members to continue where I would leave off. At my farewell party, the manager promised me I would have a job waiting for me next summer.

The next couple of semesters went by rather fast and before I knew it, summer was at my doorstep once again. I visited Rose seeking summer employment. Since I was out of the workforce and was never one for watching T.V., I did not realize our economy started to slow down during that year as we headed into a recessionary period. Rose explained the company was not doing as well in comparison to the previous year and customer orders were down. She then expressed how impressed she was with my job performance the previous summer and remembered her promise. Even though her organization had a hiring freeze, she was going to employ me for the summer regardless. She then looked at me and said "I will keep my promise". Almost twenty years have passed since I last saw Rose. I'm not sure if she realized the impact she had on a young man just starting his life. She taught me a very valuable lesson on the importance of keeping your word. Since then, I have always strived to be a man of promise.

The world is full of people trying to get ahead, sometimes at the expense of their word. To our tragedy, gone are the days of promises sealed by a handshake. A promise is a commitment. It should be viewed as a covenant or contract that is binding. With it comes an obligation to act or perform. It sets the tone of expectation for one or more persons and erodes our character if not fully kept. Might you always strive to maintain the integrity that comes from the knowledge you are only as good as your word.

CORE PRINCIPLE 10

DARE TO DREAM: RECAPTURING YOUR LIFE BY PLANNING YOUR FUTURE

"All our dreams can come true, if we have the courage to pursue them."

Walt Disney

Walt Disney is a wonderful example of a man that had passion and the courage to pursue his dreams. He was born around the turn of the 20th century on December 5th 1901. With little money, he pursued a career in art and dreamed of opening an amusement park where families could gather together. The lack of finances was not a discouragement to Walt, instead he found creative ways to seek the finances required to build a 160-acre park. Even after securing the land he was faced with countless challenges he had to overcome in order to realize his dream. After investing all his energy and effort, Disneyland opened their gates in 1955. Walt's dream finally materialized at the tender age of 53.

I have great respect for Walt Disney and have not only visited Disneyland, but several other parks that were created. Because Walt dared to dream, Disney's legacy will continue to touch the lives of millions in generations to come. I love the memories created and the energy and excitement you feel that lasts long after your visit ends. It is a place where adults can play carefree as we once did as children. A time in life when dreams, imagination and creativity were encouraged. A time when your dreams could not be dimmed or faded with life's worries and financial cares. It's time to take a stand. Decide today to breathe life back into your dreams and pursue a life worth living. Let us DARE TO DREAM.

"The future belongs to those who believe in the beauty of their dreams."

Eleanor Roosevelt

All dreams start with a vision. What are some of the things you would like to accomplish if time or money was not an obstacle? What type of car would you drive? Where would your home be located? What would you do with your spare time? What places would you like to visit? The possibilities are as endless as your imagination.

Let us have some fun! Think of all the life experiences you would like to have. Visualize them as if you have already accomplished these goals. How do they make you feel? If you feel excited, positive or happy, you are on the right path. If not, continue to do some soul searching as you build the type of life in your imagination you have always wanted to experience. As you continue to explore what it is you truly desire, it is important to dream BIG! Dreams should not be limited due to a lack of time or money. Once you have a good idea on the type of life you would like to have, create your "Dare to Dream List".

The process of writing down your dreams is important. This step requires a physical action and will give your dreams energy. It also sends a positive signal to the ever abundant universe or God source and sets your plan in motion. Once your dreams are written out, state your intentions out-loud realizing spoken words are full of creative power.

If debt freedom was not included on your list, then I want you to add it. Not having debt and operating on a cash basis is going to be critical to your success. Paying off your debt obligations will not only increase your net worth, but take you one step closer to meeting all your goals and objectives including retirement. Think of how wonderful it will be to live a life where time constraints and financial woes are not a concern. Think of the possibilities debt freedom is going to provide knowing this is going to be a reality for YOU!

After exploring your initial list, you must include the details. If you are seeking a specific outcome, then you must be specific! Without being specific and clear, your dreams become fuzzy sending mixed signals into the universe only delaying the outcome of what you truly desire. For example, if one of your desires is debt freedom, run the numbers using The Toxic Debt Solution™. Once the desired information is obtained, rewrite your goal including the details making it more specific and clear. The newly written goal might look like the following: My goal is to become debt free by following the Toxic Debt Solution™. I plan to use a Debt Freedom Factor™ of $300 per month to accomplish this goal. Notice the details. You are not only declaring your intention of being debt free, (My goal is to become debt free) but you also answered the question of "How" this is going to be accomplished. (By following The Toxic Debt Solution™).

Want even more goal clarity? Include a timetable. If possible, a timetable should include a start and finish date. If you do not have the current means to fund a specific dream, and a time table is uncertain, then put down a date you feel comfortable with. Your revised goal might look like the following: My goal is to become debt free by following The Toxic Debt Solution™. I plan to use a Debt Freedom Factor™ of $300 per month starting June 1st. By following this program, I will pay off my debts within 9 years and 3 months. Having details including timeframes will make your goals measurable and allow you to track your success as you move forward on life's journey.

Next, it is important to discover your motivational force. Motivational forces are what drives you forward and provides you with the needed energy and determination to accomplish what you set out to do. This force can be different for everyone. For some, striving to create a better life for their children might be a focus point. For others, it might include serving in their community and making a difference in the world. It does not matter what your motivational force is. As long as it calls you to action and provides you with the motivation required to move forward, embrace it! Make sure you keep your list of motivational forces along with your goals and objectives.

Prioritization is the next step. Number your dreams in order of priority based on what is important to you. Since debt freedom increases your net worth and takes you closer to achieving all your other goals and objectives, it should be pretty high on your list. After your dreams are listed in order of importance, determine if the goal can be achieved in the short term, (Under 3 years) long term (More than 7 years) or somewhere in the middle. For a lack of a better word, I typically call these the mid-term goals. (Between 3-7 years)

Since some of your goals, including debt freedom, is typically long term in nature and will take more than 7 years to accomplish, it is important to focus on achieving some of your short term goals simultaneously. Doing this will help create the balance your life requires and allow you to realize some of your dreams in the short term! I suggest you choose 3 of the short term goals most important to you. Normally, these dreams do not require a substantial amount of money to fund. Regardless of what you would like to accomplish or experience in the short term, do not allocate more than 2% of your gross monthly income towards achieving them. Following this guideline will ensure you are not going to spend too much money chasing your dreams while still in debt.

One of the very last steps required to capture your dreams is monitoring. Periodically check your progress. Are you on track toward reaching the goals and objectives in the timeframe you originally set? Life is full of financial emergencies that might take priority over some of our goals. These temporary detours are okay as long as you continue to stay focused and keep your eye on what is most important to you. Do not think you are failing if you need to adjust your plan. The only time you fail is when you give up hope and abandon your dreams. You are too important to let this happen. Make the decision today to cross the finish line and reap the rewards of a joyful life.

QUICK GUIDE TO DREAM DEVELOPMENT

1. Create your "Dare To Dream List".
2. Dreams/objectives must be specific and measurable.
3. You must include a timetable for accomplishment.
4. Keep them visible and review the list several times a week.
5. Monitor your progress and make appropriate adjustments.
6. Celebrate your success.

Congratulations! It is wonderful you took the time required to do this exercise, however if you keep this information tucked away in a note tablet, how easy we forget what is really important to us. I suggest you place your Dare to Dream List in a visible area and review them several times a week. Better yet, do as Rhonda Byrne suggested in her international Best Selling book and DVD "The Secret" and create a vision board. A vision board not only has your written goals, but should also include pictures of what you desire, inspirational quotes and anything else that inspires and motivates you.

INTERESTING STATISTICS...
(In case you were wondering)

- Studies show only 3% of people set goals.

- These 3% are more financially successful than the other 97% combined. However, I have yet to discover a reliable source or study that documents this as fact. One thing I do know. Goals provide you with direction in life and will add to your ultimate success.

- People that set goals achieve greater financial success than those who do not.

WHY SHOULD YOU SET GOALS?

1. They will provide you with motivation and the drive necessary for accomplishment.
2. Goals allow you to prioritize your time.
3. Setting goals allow you to stretch your limits and invites personal growth and development.
4. Once obtained, they will give you a sense of self worth and increase your confidence.
5. Goals will provide you with direction and allow you to focus on the things most important to you.
6. They add purpose and meaning to life.
7. Goals open up the realm of possibility providing you with increased hope for a greater tomorrow.

TOP 3 REASONS PEOPLE DO NOT SET GOALS

Be cautious never to fall into any of the following traps. They will only suppress your ability to achieve a more successful and rewarding life. Recognize if any of the following apply to you then seek to make the conscious choice not to be trapped in a life that is not fulfilling. Make the decision today you are going to move forward and accomplish all your heart's desires. By doing this you will reap the rewards of a greater tomorrow and find purpose in your life. YOU DESERVE IT!

1. **FEAR** - Fear is by far one of the greatest of all inhibitors. People fear change, success, failure, the unknown, fame, love and commitment. Fear dashes your hopes and desires and will stop you from making the changes required to move in a positive direction. By reading this book, your decision was already made. It is time to get outside your comfort zone and experience the great and glorious world which is at your doorsteps.

2. **LACK OF KNOWLEDGE** – If it is the lack of knowledge that holds you back from accomplishing your goals and objectives, then make it a priority to seek education. Replace your doubts with knowledge. This will give you the ability to move forward with confidence and provide you with a determination to succeed.

3. **NEGATIVITY** – Catch yourself from stepping into this pit of despair. The words "I can't", "I'm

not capable", and "I'm not able to" need to be removed from your vocabulary. Substitute negative phrases with positive ones. For instance, replace "If only I could" with "I could do that". Do NOT be your worse self critic. Unfortunately, there are plenty of people around that could fill that role on your behalf. Many people are drawn towards negativity. Make a decision today and decide not to be one of them. Negative people thrive in an environment where they allow themselves to play the role of a victim verse taking a stance of accountability. You are responsible for the outcome of your future! Seek positive relationships. People that will support your hopes and dreams no matter how far out of reach they might initially appear.

ANSWERS TO LIFE'S QUESTIONS

CAN SOME OF MY GOALS NOT BE FINANCIALLY BASED? YES

Goals that are financially based only represent a small portion of the ones that should be important to you. Every individual is unique and different. Goals could also include those associated with health, fitness, personal development spirituality, marriage, relationships, career development, and education. The list is endless. Remember, you are the master creator of your life. Your goals and objectives should be based on the areas you find most important.

HOW CAN I GET SPECIFIC ON SOME OF MY BIGGER GOALS WHEN I DO NOT HAVE THE MONEY TO FUND THEM?

Goals are designed to help you stretch and achieve a greater tomorrow. If you have difficulty placing a timeframe on a goal due to financial limitations, pick a date you feel comfortable with. Realize you will begin to attract the situations and circumstances into your life allowing you to obtain whatever it is you desire.

HOW DO I CHANGE INTERNALLY?

Changing internally is easy once you realize it is all a choice. What you believe about yourself including your limitations is self-imposed. You adopt many people's opinions allowing them to shape your reality and what you believe to be true. You have the capacity to change your beliefs! To do this, you must first start with an internal evaluation. Recognize any negative beliefs you might be carrying. Once they are recognized, find out where they originated from. For example, if you struggle financially and never seem to have enough money to cover your bills and daily living expenses, chances are very likely you have a negative belief about money! This negative belief you decided to adopt could have originated from a variety of places. For example, your religious upbringing might have drilled into your unconscious mind that money is the root of all evil. Since this is not your desire (being evil), you consistently make unhealthy choices as it relates to your finances. If you further explore the origins of this belief, it is not the money that is the root of evil, but the love of it. In other words, the scripture reference is telling you not to make money your God. Once you recognize and decide to change your negative beliefs and adopt positive ones, the floodgates will open and you will begin to accept and attract financial abundance and wealth into your life. This self evaluation, recognition and decision to change your unhealthy beliefs into positive ones can be done in all areas of your life that are not in harmony with whatever it is you desire. Including love! Reprogramming your unhealthy belief patterns start with awareness. Affirmations and positive thoughts have been used for thousands of years and play a critical role in the reprogramming process. Sound interesting? Then pick up a copy of my new book release entitled, Silent Reflections™. In it I share affirmations and Empowerment Thoughts™ that are designed to change your life. Access www.charlesjmachinski.com or call The Coaching Box, LLC at. 801-542-0616 for additional information.

CAN MY GOALS CHANGE? YES

It is important to remember that goals are not static, they are flexible. If your time table was unrealistic, then change the timetable. If you underestimated the finances needed to accomplish a goal, make the appropriate adjustments. Remember, goals are designed to help you grow and develop. Since you are in a constant state of change, your goals can change too.

WHAT IF I FAIL?

There is no such thing as failure, only learning opportunities. If your actions did not produce the desired outcome, evaluate your plan, make the adjustments necessary and continue to move forward. Failure only occurs when you abandon your dreams. Be tenacious! President Abraham Lincoln is a role model for us to follow. He was plagued by many of life's challenges, yet overcame these obstacles and achieved historic success. Honest Abe was born the son of a poor farmer. His mother died in his youth. At an early age, they were forced from their home due to being bankrupt. He suffered personal business failure that took years of work to recover from. As a young man he found the love of his life and was engaged to be married only to suffer a broken heart when his fiancée died before they got married. In his aspiration to run for public office, he was defeated when running for legislature, congress, and senate multiple times. The outcome? On November 6, 1860 Abe Lincoln was elected 16th President of The United States! Decide today and do what it takes to achieve success.

HOW DO I HANDLE GOALS THAT SEEM TOO LARGE TO ACCOMPLISH?

When designing an action plan required for goal attainment, create small steps or action items that must be completed to help you get there. After you finish your list, number the steps in order of importance. Also include timetables for the accomplishment of each step. Focus on the steps individually, one at a time starting with the most critical for the successful obtainment of your goal. Once a step is completed, follow the order of priority until your goal is reached.

TIPS FOR A MORE REWARDING AND FULFILLING LIFE

SELF RECOGNITION

We must not only recognize our successes, but the learning opportunities most people might consider failures.

"Failure is success if we learn from it."

Malcolm Forbes

Not achieving a desired outcome only presents a learning opportunity, a time to grow and develop. If a desired outcome was not obtained, you have the capacity to make the appropriate adjustments and change your course of action to achieve success. The lack of desire or willingness to change will only prolong your existing state and inhibit your professional and spiritual well being. Make the choice today and embrace change!

"We can't become what we need to be by remaining what we are."

Oprah Winfrey

BONUS MATERIAL "A"

ANSWERS AND COMMENTS TO LIFE'S GENERAL QUESTIONS

THE FAMILY VEHICLE... YOU ARE NOT WHAT YOU DRIVE.

The statistics are staggering on how much money consumers spend on brand new car purchases. Even more heart wrenching is the amount a car depreciates in value the moment you drive it off the dealer's lot. In most cases, it takes a couple of years worth of payments just to hit the break even mark where you might be able to sell the car for what you owe the bank. Remember, be wise with all your purchases and recognize you are not what you drive. This section is designed to answer questions you might have about the family vehicle.

MY CAR IS ON ITS LAST LEG, SHOULD I BUY A NEW ONE?

Remember, our goal is to be and remain debt free. Unless your car is about to give up the ghost and is heading toward the car graveyard, make every attempt possible to delay your purchase. **DO NOT RATIONALIZE!** I have heard time and time again that car repairs would exceed the cost of a new vehicle purchase. Even if your car needed a total makeover and cost $3000 to fix, would you rather pay that or 5 years worth of payments? For example, let us assume the average vehicle purchase has a sticker price of $18,500.

With a 5% note rate over a 5 year period, you would have a monthly obligation of about $350! Based on this number, if you applied your monthly payment towards the $3000 it would cost to fix your existing vehicle, it would be paid off in a little under 9 months. Now I'm not saying there is never a time for a new vehicle purchase. My goal is to make you think and run the numbers. Once you run the numbers and could honestly say a purchase makes sense, then go for it! Ideally, any vehicle purchase should be made with cash. However, for most people still struggling to pay off debts or that do not have the liquidity for a cash purchase, credit might be your only option. Shop around for the best interest rate and try to minimize your car loan to a 2-3 year period. One last thought. You should NEVER purchase a brand new car. According to an article featured on an MSN website, Consumer Reports stated most models typically lose about 45% of their value in the first 3 years! Before you decide on a purchase, do your homework. Consumer Reports offers an array of reports and information including vehicle comparisons, value, reliability and other tips. A site to determine value is Kelly Blue Book at www.kbb.com. CARFAx is another resource to ensure you are going to make a wise purchase. This company searches databases nationwide using the vehicles VIN number and provides a vehicle history that might uncover issues a seller might try to hide. Their site can be accessed at www.carfax.com

DOES IT EVER MAKE SENSE TO LEASE A VEHICLE? NO

Purchasing a vehicle on a lease would be like buying a home with an interest only note. You will never own it and it costs you a fortune in payments. I'm speaking from personal experience. I was foolish enough to acquire a car on an open ended lease which gave me the option to purchase the vehicle at the end of my payments. The terms of the contract were quite strict. I was limited in the amount of miles I could drive on an annual basis. To increase my miles from 12k to 18k cost me a few thousand dollars in payments over a 5 year period. The contract also set forth extensive charges and fees associated with an early termination if I chose to trade the vehicle in before the lease ended. Once my lease contract was about to expire, the buyout amount along with additional fees was going to cost me $7k. Of course, I did not have an option but to purchase the vehicle since I was thousands of miles over my contractual limit and the lender was going to charge me .18 cents per mile if I returned the car. This excluded any other cost due to wear and tear the lender did not consider normal. The unfortunate thing is that lenders are ultra conservative on what they consider normal. In my case, if you had more than one scratch on the same panel, it was cause for replacement! Once you add up all the dings and scratches along with the over mileage charges, most people would have to pay thousands of dollars just for the lender to take the car off your hands! If you add up the costs of a purchase option and add this sum to the total lease payments made, chances are you paid thousands of dollars more for the vehicle beyond the sticker price. My suggestion if you need a car? Buy a good used vehicle within your financial means and stay away from lease options like you would the plague.

I CAN NO LONGER AFFORD MY CAR? WHAT SHOULD I DO? THE ANSWER IS SIMPLE... DUMP IT

Besides a home, a car is one of the most expensive purchases you could make. According to an article in Kiplinger's Personal Finance Magazine, the average down payment for a vehicle in the United States is $2400, the average amount financed is $24,864 and the average monthly payment is $479. Based on these numbers, the average American is paying $5,748 annually for their car! Assuming you are in the 28% tax bracket, you have to make over $7,300 per year in gross income to cover this debt obligation. It is time to relieve yourself of this financial drain and burden. If there is enough equity in the vehicle, sell the car on your own. Place a 4-sale sign in the window and do everything in your power to get rid of it. Explore other marketing options including on-line exposure. www.craigslist.com is a wonderful website to start. However, you might want to limit the sale to your local area and make it clear in your ad the buyer is responsible for the vehicle pickup. The money you receive from this transaction should go towards the purchase of a reliable used car that is more economical. If possible, do not purchase another one. If your household has multiple cars, work out a family share plan.

If you owe more than the car is worth and do not have the liquidity to purchase something else, you might want to consider trading it in at a dealership. The difference of what is owed verses the trade in value could be financed and rolled into the loan of a more affordable car. Remember, do your homework! Know the approximate value of your car before you coordinate with a dealership. Better yet, when doing your research by accessing a site like Kelly Blue Book, print out the value page and bring it with you.

One last thought. Run the numbers and see how much money this change would free up, then do what makes financial sense.

SHOULD I PAY CASH FOR AN ESSENTIAL ITEM (LIKE A CAR) IF IT EMPTIES MY BANK ACCOUNT? NO

Operating on a cash basis is critical to achieving financial success. However, it does not make sense to empty your account and leave yourself without an emergency buffer. For example, let's assume you have no other choice but to purchase a car. After searching around, you determine the cost of a good used vehicle is $7500. You could pay cash for the car, but it would totally empty your accounts. Do not do this! Instead, put $4500 cash towards the vehicle and leave yourself with $3k emergency money. Finance the difference with a loan program offering you the most favorable interest rate. Then pay the note off as quickly as you can.

SHOULD I CO-SIGN FOR A LOVED ONE THAT NEEDS A CAR? NO

If you ignore my advice and decide to co-sign for someone expect to make the payments and stay in debt that much longer. There are reasons dear friends or family members are not able to secure a loan for themselves. Often it is due to a lack of fiscal responsibility and the person's credit is not at levels required to obtain that type of financing. Even scarier is their income levels against their existing debt obligations are too high when seeking to obtain additional financing. Simply put: THEY CAN NOT AFFORD IT! My word of advice? DO NOT DO IT! You will not only save money, but family relationships and friends. If you have the financial means to assist them without causing you financial hardship, fantastic! But consider the money a gift not a loan.

IF YOU THINK EDUCATION IS EXPENSIVE, TRY IGNORANCE

"Before anything else, getting ready is the secret of success."

Henry Ford

Statistics from a variety of website resources differ. According to a salary profile from www.indeed.com, the national high average salary for a college graduate is close to $63,000 a year. According to www.earnmydegree.com, on average a person with a master's degree earns a little over $31,000 more annually than a high school graduate. This statistic is further supported by a study conducted by the United States

Census Bureau. Even if these statistics are relatively low, history dictates that obtaining a quality education is pivotal to achieving financial success. To demonstrate the critical role an education has on your income level, let's be very conservative and assume the average college graduate makes only $15,000 more annually than a high school graduate. On a monthly basis, this would bring in a gross income equivalent to $1250. If a person was to invest this difference and received an average rate of return of 10% annually over a 20 year period, this money would grow substantially. In fact, the total dollar value after a 20 year investment would equal $949,211.04! Let's compare this figure to the cost of obtaining an education. According to the College Board, the average cost of an education from a state institution is a little over $6,500 annually. Over the course of a four year period, the total spent would amount up to a little over $26,000. Its' safe to assume that within the first couple of years after graduation the extra income earned because of your degree would exceed the full cost of tuition you paid to obtain an education. Many of us are fortunate enough to be living in nations that foster and encourage higher learning. A vital part of our human experience is our ability to seek and strive for greater knowledge and wisdom. Education is the prerequisite required to produce a greater tomorrow. If you think education is expensive, try ignorance.

This section is designed to assist you and your loved ones by providing resources and answers to questions related to continuing education.

1. **Get involved when your child is choosing a University.** Starting at a local community college or deciding to attend a state school verses a private university could save you THOUSANDS of dollars. According to the College Board, the average price tag for a private university is $25,143. For a public education, the average price tag is only $6,585. For great values, access www.kiplingger.com Click on "Your Money" then "Best College Values".

2. **Apply for financial aid at perspective schools early and compare the award received.** You will find that aid varies by institution. Some will have the ability to offer grant money which is given to students as a gift and is not expected to be paid back. This is much better than a package whose primary component is made up of educational loans. www.finaid.org is a great place to start. This site has information on scholarships, loans, savings plans and other forms of aid that might be available.

3. **Take the time necessary and search out scholarships, internships, grants and loans.** Statistics show there is close to $143 Billion Dollars in financial aid available for students. http://apps.collegeboard ss/welcome.jsp Is an excellent website. They have lots of tools and information for perspective students and their parents.

4. **Set the expectation up front.** If you have the financial means, allocate a certain dollar amount to assist your children with paying for an education. Let them know in advance what you

are capable of contributing and do not go beyond this budgeted amount.

5. **Open a 529 plan and start investing for your children's education. (But only if you are financially capable and not at the expense of your retirement planning)** A 529 plan is named after the Internal Revenue code which created these plans back in the late 90s. Contributions to the plan are not tax deductable, but distributions to cover the cost of education are federally tax free under the Pension Protection Act of 2006. For more information, access: www.savingforcollege.com.

SHOULD I INCLUDE A STUDENT LOAN IN THE TOXIC DEBT SOLUTION™? MAYBE

Student loans typically carry one of the lowest interest rates. That being said, it usually is the cheapest money you will ever borrow. Most of the time, you would be able to get a higher rate of return if you applied this money toward investing. If this is the case, then do not include it. Pay the minimal monthly payment until the note is satisfied and enjoy the continued growth of your investment portfolio.

IS IT OKAY TO CO-SIGN FOR A LOAN IF IT IS USED FOR EDUCATIONAL PURPOSES? YES

If your child is responsible and serious about the education they are seeking to obtain, then it is okay to co-sign for a loan. However, you must be quite clear on how much assistance you can afford to provide them. All too often I have seen parents needlessly struggle trying to provide aid to their children at the expense of their own financial security. Do not sacrifice your retirement investment or emergency fund to cover the cost of a child's education. You would be more of a burden to them later in life if you needed to rely upon them financially in the future.

RECHARGE YOUR BATTERIES... TRIPS, VACATIONS AND FAMILY OUTINGS

The Toxic Debt Solution™ is a process that is not going to happen overnight. Often, it takes discipline and sometimes several years to pay off all your debt obligations in their entirety. You must seek balance in your life. Balance is critical if you desire to maintain mental and physical health. People need to occasionally recharge their batteries by taking a trip, vacation or family outing and you are no different!

SHOULD I DELAY GOING ON VACATION UNTIL I PAY OFF MY DEBTS? NO (But here are 20 guidelines and tips you should follow)

1. Before you plan a little getaway, ensure you have a $1k-$3k emergency fund. This fund is not to be used for your trip or any other non-emergency.
2. Avoid expensive vacations and plan within your means. Remember, every dollar you spend is a precious resource so use your money wisely.
3. Consider cheaper alternatives like visiting National Parks. The National Park System has 391

areas and covers over 84 million acres. For more information access www.NPS.gov.

4. You are not required to pay full price when attending a museum. Museums are a nonprofit organization and the price listed is a suggested donation. If you have the financial means to donate, please do and cut your travel related costs elsewhere. If not, advise the cashier how much of a donation your family can afford.

5. If your destination includes flights, travel on Tuesday or Wednesday to minimize airfare costs. For local travel, search online and use regional carriers for additional savings.

6. Advise the airline gate agent you would be interested in getting bumped if the flight is in an overflow capacity. (Overbooked) A few extra hours of your time could give you a free flight for future use and a possible meal.

7. Use online providers to comparison shop.

www.priceline.com

www.orbitz.com

www.vacationstogo.com

www.expedia.com

www.hotwire.com

www.travelocity.com

www.kayak.com

www.lastminute.com

www.momondo.com

When making hotel reservations directly, ask for a discount. Also inquire how much the same room might be on a different day of the week. Better yet, stay with family or friends.

8. Stay in a hotel that not only offers the best rate and services, but one that offers free breakfast. This could save quite a bit of money especially if you are traveling as a family.

9. If your travel plans are flexible, search airlines sites for last minute deals.

10. If you are a member of a club or affiliation that offers travel related discounts, use them.

11. If you are a member in the armed forces, a student or senior citizen, ask for a discount.

12. Pack snacks when traveling. (Especially when visiting tourist areas where the cost of food is very expensive) Having snacks will curtail hunger as well as your spending.

13. Search on-line and look for money saving coupons. Just a little amount of time surfing the web could save you quite a bit of money.

14. Planning a trip in advance? Purchase an Entertainment Book for the area you plan to visit. This book is filled with valuable coupons and generous offers. It could be worth the money even if a repeat visit is not in your current travel plans. At the end of the trip, donate the book to a local who might enjoy longer term savings.
www.entertainment.com

15. Check with your insurance provider to see if damages to a rental car are covered in the event of

a mishap. If your travel plans are not business related, most providers will cover you. If you are covered, waive the insurance option at the rental counter and keep the money where it belongs. In your pocket!

16. If needed, a weekly car rental will save quite a bit of money than an average daily rate.

17. Do not use a Taxi. Walk or use weekly passes for mass transit.

18. Travel in a group and split the costs.

19. Scan sites like e-Bay, Craigslist and Amazon for good deals on lodging and event ticket sales. Since you will be purchasing from an on-line seller, if possible, check their sales rating. The higher the rating, the safer you should feel about your purchase.

DOES OWNING A TIMESHARE MAKE FINANCIAL SENSE? NO

Organizations that promote or offer timeshares have very trained professionals that thrive in a high pressure sales environment. Even the most thrifty and frugal might fall victim to their game. First, these organizations entice potential customers by offering an array of gifts. In my teens, I allowed myself to get lured into a presentation. I originally thought "what could I lose with the exception of a couple hours during my vacation?" Besides, I was promised a Mexican blanket, $20 Pesos and a free breakfast buffet. It was not long after our arrival that my cousin and I were attacked by the ravaging wolves (also known as timeshare sales professionals). I was quite shocked when the gentleman assigned as our consultant sat himself down at our table when we were in middle of eating breakfast. (They could not even wait until we were finished!) Most timeshares are a waste of money and have far too many restrictions. You pay thousands of dollars for the right to use a property on a restricted basis. Sometimes if you do not use your designated week(s), you lose them. Besides, do you really think you will visit that exact location during the same week for the next twenty years? Regardless as to how flexible a program may appear, there are always additional fees to take into consideration. Some fees might include maintenance, booking and transfer costs that could easily run up to a few hundred dollars on an annual basis. One last thing to think about, If timeshares where such a great investment, then why are so many people looking to sell them?

Need to sell a timeshare?

www.sellmytimesahrenow.com or call: 1-877-815-4227

www.sellmytimeshare.com

www.buymytimeshare.com

THE CONSEQUENCES OF NOT PAYING UP

For every action, there is an associated outcome and this holds true when you stop paying your creditors and head into default. Not all creditors will go through the expense of suing you for payment. Just because a judgment is received does not guarantee them payment, especially if the consumer seeks protection from their creditors by filing a bankruptcy claim. However, for accounts with high balances, it is usually an option they tend to explore. This section is designed to answer the most commonly asked questions on the consequences of not paying up.

CAN A CREDITOR GARNISH MY WAGES? YES

A garnishment is a court order directing your employer to withhold earnings so they can be applied to the debts that you owe. In order for a creditor to garnish your wages, they must seek a judgment through the court system. If you are served papers due to a pending lawsuit, it is not in your best interest to ignore them. If possible, consult with an attorney. Once granted, a judgment will show up on your credit report and remain open until the debt is satisfied. Even after the obligation is satisfied, all judgments will remain on your credit report for a 7 year period.

CAN A CREDITOR FREEZE MY CHECKING ACCOUNT? YES

It is totally legal for a creditor to freeze and attach your accounts for money that is owed them. This is accomplished though our court system when a judgment is granted. To limit the amount they can collect at one time, be sure you are present at the hearing so a judge hears your case. It is important to know social security funds or money received from a variety of public assistance programs are exempt and can't be frozen and used to pay off your debt obligations. However, if you do not show up for court, the judge will not be aware of the origin of this money and might grant an attachment on your accounts.

ARE THERE ANY IMPLICATIONS IF I SETTLE MY ACCOUNTS WITH MY CREDITORS AND NOT PAY THE FULL AMOUNT OWED? YES

If you have negotiated a compromise or settlement agreement with a creditor, you may be liable for taxes on the portion of your debt that was not paid. Your creditor can "write-off" the outstanding balance and claim it as a tax loss to the IRS. When this is done, you will receive a 1099-C: Cancelation of Debt form. This indicates your creditor is going to write off the unpaid part of your liability. The full dollar amount of the write off is considered income which you must include on your taxes! In addition to possible tax liability, your credit report and rating will be impacted since the accounts will not be reflected as paid in full, but satisfied.

DO YOU ALWAYS HAVE TO PAY TAXES WHEN YOU RECEIVE A 1099-C CANCELLATION OF DEBT? DEPENDS

Insolvency is one of the only situations where the IRS will waive your tax obligation. Insolvency occurs when your total assets do not exceed your total debt obligations

For additional information and reporting guidelines, contact the IRS.

WHAT IRS FORM DO I NEED TO FILL OUT IF I AM INSOLVENT?

To prove insolvency to the IRS, you must fill out Form 982: Reduction of Tax Attributes Due to Discharge of Indebtedness. To further prove your case, I suggest you attach a letter of explanation highlighting the reasons behind your current financial situation and how you derived at the calculations stated on your Form 982.

WHAT IS A BANKRUPTCY?

There are two different types of bankruptcy; both are coordinated on a federal court level. A Chapter 13 is a debt repayment plan where the court determines the amount you are obligated to pay your creditors on a monthly basis. Once the specified time period is over, the remaining balances on your accounts are dismissed. A Chapter 7 occurs when a Federal Court judge dismisses your outstanding debt obligations giving you a fresh start free from financial worry. If your financial situation is desperate and you need to explore bankruptcy as a potential option, contact an attorney that offers a free consultation.

DOES IT EVER MAKE SENSE TO DECLARE BANKRUPTCY? SOMETIMES

Long term sickness, death of a spouse or loved one and extended periods of unemployment might contribute to this move. There are many legitimate reasons, so try not to feel embarrassed if you need to explore this option.

Things will get better and this might be a key towards financial healing and recapturing your mental sanity. However, bankruptcy was never designed with the intent of relieving someone from their financial burden resulting from a lack of discipline and overspending. Since you are responsible for your outstanding debt obligations, bankruptcy should be your very last option. You need to make every attempt to pay off the debts you have accumulated. Make every adjustment possible to free up money and apply it towards The Toxic Debt Solution™. If after all your adjustments, you are not able to survive and still financially upside down, consult an attorney for a free consultation.

DO I HAVE TO SELL MY HOME OR CAR IF I DECLARE BANKRUPTCY? MAYBE

Under a Chapter 7 Bankruptcy, if it is determined your car or home exceeds a certain net value the courts can demand that you liquidate the assets to pay your creditors. The total net value will vary by state, so check with a legal professional for exact details.

DOES A BANKRUPTCY PROTECT ME FROM MY CREDITORS? YES

Bankruptcy code 326(a) is known as the automatic stay. Once you file for bankruptcy, and advise your creditors, collection efforts and any form of harassment will cease. However, it does not always protect your assets.

HOW CAN I HAVE CREDITORS STOP HARRASING ME IF I DO NOT APPLY FOR BANKRUPTCY?

The Federal Fair Debt Collection Practices Act forbids creditors from contacting you directly at your request. The law also states they can only call you between the hours of 8am - 9pm and can't threaten you by stating they are going to raise your interest rates and charge you additional fees. If a collection agency is in violation of this Act, you can file a complaint with the Federal Trade Commission. www.ftc.gov In addition to filing a formal complaint, you should send a certified letter to the collection agency that has violated your rights. In the letter, detail when and how your rights were violated.

ASSET PROTECTION AND ESTATE PLANNING

Accumulating wealth is a process. Unless, of course, you are fortunate enough to have a long lost relative leave you their fortune. (Personally, I would not bank on this as a possibility) Regardless of how your riches are accumulated, you must seek to protect and safeguard your assets. A will and trust are a couple of safeguards designed to provide you with the protection you need.

AT WHAT AGE SHOULD I HAVE A WILL? 18 AND BEYOND

A will is one of the safeguards you need to have in order to protect your family. A will provides direction on how your estate is to be distributed upon your death. If you die without having a will, you are said to have died intestate. When this occurs, the courts decide how your assets are distributed and who will be granted custody over your children. This process could be long and quite expensive. The benefits of having a will include your personal appointment of guardianship for children, a trustee and executor. There are many will writing software packages available. Some are even stocked on the shelves at your local office supply store. Online options would include LegalZoom and Nolo.

Legal Zoom - www.LegalZoom.com

Nolo – www.nolo.com

WHAT IS A TRUST?

A living trust is recognized as a legal entity and designed to protect your estate. Having a trust will help your estate avoid probate which is the legal process of distributing your assets upon your death. A trust allows your assets to be distributed quickly to your heirs saving time and money. There are different types of trusts each offering a variety of benefits designed for your protection.

A) **LIVING TRUST** – This is the most common form of trust designed to protect your assets including your home and investment accounts. A revocable living trust can be changed at any time which makes it flexible. This trust is also easy to set up and maintain.

B) **QTIP TRUST** – This trust is also known as a Qualified Terminable Interest Property Trust. It is ideal for people who want to provide for their spouses financial needs while they are alive, but want their assets distributed to their children or other third parties organizations upon their death. This might be a perfect trust for people who marry later in life, but have children from a previous relationship.

C) **BYPASS TRUST** – This trust is ideal for married couples who want to do their estate planning together. This trust might have tax benefits associated with it by allowing assets to be transferred to the surviving spouse without taxation.

D) **IRREVOCABLE INSURANCE TRUST** - is a trust that can't be changed once created. This trust is designed to protect the value of your life insurance policy by avoiding estate taxation.

E) **CHARITABLE UNI TRUST** – Was created in 1969 by congress. This trust allows you to donate assets to charity thereby providing you with large tax advantages. It also allows you and your loved ones to draw an income off the trust until your death when the principal balance of the trust gets passed to designated charities. Just like the ILIT, this trust is considered irrevocable limiting changes that can be made once set up.

Since the distribution of assets can vary by state law and you want to ensure your assets are protected, I suggest you contact an estate planning attorney to explore the options that best meet your needs. I do not recommend you use an online service to set up a trust.

ARE LIFE INSURANCE PROCEEDS TAXABLE? YES

Insurance proceeds received are free from income tax, but not estate tax. This usually impacts the wealthy only since simple estates are not required by the IRS to file an estate tax return. (Check with the IRS for details)

OUR GOOD OL' UNCLE SAM: TAXATION

According to the Tax Foundation, tax freedom day was the second week of April. This means every dollar the average American earned for the first 3 ½ months of the year will go towards your tax liability. It's safe to assume some people will pay more in taxes on an annual basis than in payments for shelter, utilities, water, sewer and trash collection combined! Always search for ways to defray this huge expense that only chips away at your net worth and your ability to meet your financial goals and objectives. Looking for a good read or education on taxation? Sandy Botkin is a well known authority and author on this subject. He is President and founder of The Tax Reduction Institute. (www.taxreductioninstitute.com) His work includes The Tax Strategies for Business Professionals and Lower Your Taxes - Big Time.

I GET QUITE A BIT OF MONEY EVERY YEAR FROM A TAX REFUND. SHOULD I APPLY ALL THIS MONEY TOWARDS DEBT? NO

First, I want you to be prepared for a financial emergency. You should have $1k-$3k in an account for that purpose. Once you have these funds, all remaining money should be used toward your debt obligations. Of course you are more than welcome to spend a little on a mini vacation or date night with your loved ones. Remember the program is not meant to make you feel so thrifty and frugal that you can't occasionally go to dinner or a movie.

IF I FILE JOINTLY WITH MY SPOUSE AM I RESPONSIBLE FOR THE BACK TAXES THEY OWE? YES

Filing a joint return with your spouse would make you obligated to pay the back taxes owed even if it was not your liability. (Per the IRS, you would be 50% liable for the previous debt).

IF I OWE TAXES, SHOULD I FILE AN EXTENTION UNTIL I HAVE THE MONEY TO PAY THEM? NO

If you do not file by the April 15th deadline and you owe taxes, you may have to pay an additional penalty for failure to file unless you can show reasonable cause that prevented you from filing. According to IRS Topic 653, (which can be accessed at www.irs.gov) Interest is charged on any unpaid tax from the due date until payment is received. The interest rate changes every 3 months and is the sum of the federal short term rate plus 3%. This interest is compounded daily! Even if you file on time, the IRS will charge you a late payment penalty assessed on a monthly basis until your tax obligation is paid in full. This penalty could go up to 25%! Bottom line, file your taxes on time and do everything in your power to pay what you owe.

WHAT OPTIONS DO I HAVE IF I FILE MY TAXES ON TIME, BUT DO NOT HAVE THE MONEY TO PAY WHAT IS OWED?

You have the option of setting up a monthly payment plan with the IRS by filing Form 9465. However, with this payment agreement, interest and penalties will continue to accumulate until the debt is paid off in its entirety. And as we mentioned above, this could be quite costly and delay your ability to pay this obligation off in full. Your best bet is to explore other options:

Alternate Option 1: Get another job. This could be a part time job just to cover this expense. Continue to work until the obligation is paid in full. Better yet, continue to work after the taxes are paid then apply the money earned toward The Toxic Debt Solution™.

Alternate Option 2: Use a low interest rate credit card or loan to pay them off. I would prefer you take this course of action verses a payment arrangement with the government which would only cost you more in the long run.

Alternate Option 3: Borrow against your 401k, but ONLY as a last resort. With this option, you pay yourself back with interest. Normally the money borrowed must be paid back within a five year period. However, it is important to know that any voluntary or involuntary separation from your employer will cause the remaining balance to become due immediately. If you do not have the funds to cover this debt, it will be considered as income and subject to taxation and a 10% early withdrawal penalty.

Notice none of my options included borrowing money from family members or friends. If you have been fiscally irresponsible, do not place your financial burdens on your loved ones. All too often I have seen animosity build up as the recipient defaults on the terms of the loan a loved one was generous enough to provide. Why destroy these relationships?

I NORMALLY GET A LARGE REFUND ON AN ANNUAL BASIS, WHAT CAN I DO SO THE GOVERNMENT TAKES OUT LESS TAXES FROM MY PAYCHECK?

Form W-4 is your personal allowance worksheet. On this worksheet a tax payer claims the amount of dependents they have. The more dependents you claim, the less taxes the government will take out of your paycheck. To make these adjustments, contact your human resource coordinator or payroll manager. However, one word of CAUTION, you do not want to place yourself in a situation where you owe taxes to the government. Before making any changes, use IRS Pub 919 to see how the amount you are having withheld compares to your projected tax obligation. This publication also discusses the details on how to adjust your tax withholding.

CHARITY: THE HIDDEN SECRET TO A TRULY REWARDING LIFE

There are so many non-profit organizations to choose from. Search out a charity and support a cause you hold dear. Donating your personal resources including time and money will enrich your life and at the same time make a positive difference in the world. Not to mention how good you will feel too.

SHOULD I STOP PAYING TITHES AND OTHER OFFERINGS IF I STILL HAVE DEBT? NO

This is one area not open for negotiation. If you are to expect continued blessings and abundance, you must pay your tithing. Once you are on the road to financial recovery and your income continues to increase, so should your charitable contributions. If you are not a church going individual, then select a reputable organization or charity and give generously.

CAN I DEDUCT ALL MY CHARITABLE CONTRIBUTIONS ON MY TAX RETURN? MAYBE

In order to deduct a contribution, it must be made to a qualified organization and not set aside for use by a specific person or individual. Generally speaking most non-profit organizations would be considered a qualified organization. Deductions are generally limited to 50%. This means your deduction for total contributions made can't exceed 50% of your total adjusted gross income. However, income and other regulations can change your allowable deduction amount, so I suggest you read Publication 526 on Charitable Contributions found on the IRS website.

WHERE CAN I FIND A REPUTABLE WEBSITE TO SEARCH AND COMPARE CHARITIES?

www.charitynavigator.org is a wonderful site filled with lots of information. You can filter your search results and view charities by rating, size, and scope of their work. This site also has great tips, articles and a hot topic section that highlights certain charities dealing with highly visible issues.

BONUS MATERIAL "B"

ADDITIONAL TIPS FOR A MORE REWARDING AND FULFULLING LIFE

YOU ARE NOT THE VICTIM

Life is full of wonderful and sometimes painful learning experiences. However, you must never play the role of the victim. Every time you do only diminishes your self-worth and allows you to place blame on others for your less than desirable situation. Take control by accepting responsibility! Where you are at in life is because of the choices you have made. If you are not leading a satisfied and rewarding life, always remember you have the power to make the changes internally and externally and choose something different.

DO NOT ADOPT OTHER PEOPLE'S NEGATIVE BELIEF PATTERNS

Our belief patterns stem from life experiences. Who we think we are and what we are capable of achieving, is typically the outcome of other people's opinion. Unfortunately, the world is full of imperfect people on their own life's journey. Take control! Formulate your own opinion and believe you are capable of accomplishing great and glorious things.

CHANGE YOUR THOUGHTS

Before anything is created or an experience realized, it was first developed by your thoughts. If your thoughts are not taking you on the type of journey you desire, then consciously decide to change them.

VOCABULARY ELIMINATION

Be careful what you say. Your words are powerful and full of creative energy. To speak with power, you must never complain, swear or speak ill of another. Learn to appreciate and accept people for who they are and what they are capable of doing at this stage in their life.

FACE YOUR DEMONS

In our personal journey, we have all done something below our standard of excellence. The outcome of some of those experiences might bring about feelings of unworthiness, worthlessness or a sense of guilt. Face your demons. If necessary, seek forgiveness and provide restitution. More importantly, you must forgive yourself. Remember, we are all imperfect people in this together.

RECOGNIZE YOUR DIVINE NATURE

All of us were created by and in the image of deity. We are co-creators with God and capable of achieving glorious things.

THE POWER OF MENTAL VISUALIZATION

Think yourself towards prosperity and the level of success you want to achieve. Dream it, Want it, Live it. The power of thought and intention is a precursor to the physical manifestation of your desires.

FOLLOW YOUR INNER GUIDE

Promptings, an inner nudge, enlightened thoughts and impressions are all Gods way of communicating and directing your path. Do not miss out on an opportunity that is yours for the taking. When inspiration strikes, do NOT wait!

REPLACE JEALOUSY WITH GRADITUTE

Jealously comes in many forms but is rooted in pride. Why can't I have that? Why don't I make as much money? What makes them so special? Get rid of your pride and start thinking about other people. Instead of being jealous when someone acquires riches, recognition or experiences something you desire, be grateful and happy for that person. This act alone will send a positive signal into the universe and open you up to receiving more positive experiences in return. So the next time envy or jealousy surfaces, recognize it is counterproductive for what you are trying to accomplish and will only delay the type of life you truly desire to attract for yourself.

TO THINE OWN SELF BE TRUE

Do not let other people direct your life and take you away from accomplishing what you truly desire. If other people's choices are not in harmony with what you are trying to accomplish, be committed and stick to your own path. Not sticking to your own path will only cause imbalance, a lack of harmony and ultimately unhappiness.

KEEP YOUR COMMITMENTS

Make a promise today to keep your commitments. Keeping them is a sign of dependability and fosters trust.

REPLACE NEGATIVE EMOTIONS

Any form of hate, malice, envy, or strife will rob you of your energy and is negative. How can you move forward in a positive direction when you do not display positive actions or have positive thoughts? You can't! Decide today to be positive and something magical will occur. You will attract more positive people and situations into your life. It will be these people that are willing and capable of helping you on your own life's journey towards success.

CHANGE YOUR PERCEPTION

Choose not to feel bad about a life experience. When you change your perception, you change your attitude and ultimately the way you feel inside. Remember, every experience is a growing opportunity. We need to learn from them.

REACH BEYOND MEASURE

Welcome the feelings associated with uncertainty. Any lofty goal worthy of achieving is designed to stretch your limits and forces you to reach beyond your measure. It is only when you allow yourself to pass over the threshold of your knowledge that you experience growth and personal development. How can you continue to evolve and create a better life without embracing change? You can't.

ADDITIONAL RESOURCES TO INSPIRE, MOTIVATE, EDUCATE AND CHANGE YOUR LIFE...

EMPOWERMENT COACHING™

You are not destined to live a life of financial hardship and difficulty!

If you desire to fast track your success and personal development, **Empowerment Coaching**™ is the answer. These affordable private teleconference sessions with the author will provide you with the individual attention and direction you need to reclaim and live the life of your dreams!

We offer a variety of coaching packages based on your needs and circumstances. For details, contact Charlie at 801-688-6789 or access www.charlesjmachinski.com

SPEAKING ENGAGEMENTS

Develop Wealth & Abundance * Find Your Passion in Life * Learn to Set & Obtain Goals * Live the Life of Your Dreams * Learn How to Keep Your Life in Harmony & Balance * Increase Sales * Improve Corporate Morale * Foster Healthy Relationships * Facilitate a Positive Work Environment * Build Self Esteem *

Our unique programs are designed based on your corporate or organizational needs. For details, contact Charlie at 801-688-6789 or access our website online at www.charlesjmachinski.com

EMPOWERMENT SERIES™

If you are not ready for private coaching sessions, we offer web based instruction. During these sessions, Charlie will motivate, inspire and provide you with the valuable insights and tools required to take your life to a heightened level of success.

Contact Charlie at 801-688-6789 for additional information or access www.charlesjmachinski.com

LOOKING TO EMPOWER YOUR COMPANY OR ORGANIZATION?

Provide them with the tools required for financial success!

We offer a quantity discount on book purchases. With volume purchases, you can coordinate a cameo appearance with the author and book signing.

For additional information, contact Charlie at 801-688-6789 or access www.charlesjmachinski.com

INTRODUCING:

Silent Reflections™
A Book of Affirmations and thoughts designed to bring you unlimited prosperity and abundance.

Affirmations have been used for thousands of years. From ancient civilizations to our modern day, the world's greatest thinkers and most successful people have used affirmations to alter the way they think and feel about who they are and what they are capable of achieving.

If you suffer from a life of mediocrity and continuously find yourself in less than desirable circumstances, the time for change is now, and that change must first be made on the inside! How can you attract opportunity, financial abundance and love if you have a belief pattern that does not support these desires? You can't! Consistent use of affirmations and empowerment thoughts is the key to reprogramming your limiting belief patterns. Once you allow yourself to adopt a new empowered way of thinking, the world and every gift it has to offer, is yours for the taking.

Pick up a copy today at:

www.charlesjmachinski.com

Cover Design By: Dean R. Vigyikan

www.deanvigyikan.com

Photography By: Nicole Ekberg

http://photobynicole.blogspot.com

THE END

www.ingramcontent.com/pod-product-compliance
Lightning Source LLC
Chambersburg PA
CBHW060554200326
41521CB00007B/571